RECONSTRUCTED CENSUS OF CESSNAS

1720-1820

Second Edit

By

C.W. Cissna

House of Cessna Publishing

June 2016
Albuquerque, New Mexico

2nd Edit
June 2021

ISBN-13: 978-1532938610
ISBN-10: 1532938616

**Cover photo by
Think Harris Photography**

Available at

Houseofcessna.com

Amazon.com

OUR AMERICA SERIES
One Family's 300-Year Saga

1: *Bury My Children in a Strange Land: 2011*
   In 1718, John and Stephen Cessna followed their Huguenot Refugee father from Ireland to a new world.

2: *Forgotten Courage: 2011*
   Stephen Cessna/Cissna struggled to be a patriot during the Revolutionary War and in every part of his life. A heroic common man was tossed in the storm of Early American Politics.

3: *The Reluctant American: 2010*
   Joseph Cessna/Cissna protected his family and neighbors in the bloodiest part of the American Revolution. Then he helped establish the State of Michigan.

4: *Let Me Live in Peace: 2012*
   The life of Col. Charles Cessna, a patriot caught in bitter politics after the American Revolution. After the War he helped develop frontier communities in Georgia, Kentucky and Mississippi.

5: *Will This Country Survive? 2013*
   Sergeant Charles Cissna and many more of our family kept the country from falling apart during the second war with England.

6: *Where Can We Prosper?   2014*
   The economic depression of the 1830s sent the family west, to virgin lands in Illinois. They were part of building the first National Road.

7: *A Nation and Family Divided: 2015*
   An anthology of various Cessnas who took part in both sides of the Civil War.

8: *Civilizing a Pioneer Generation: 2018*
   The assassination of Sheriff George Sisney ended a family feud. Indian Agent John Cisney investigated the massacre at Wounded Knee and stopped uprisings in Colorado and Wisconsin.

This is a history of America as experienced by one family through ten generations and three centuries.

RESEARCH BOOKS AVAILABLE

House of Cessna, Book One: A reprint of Howard Cessna's work from 1901, including commentaries and corrections.

House of Cessna, Book Two: A reprint of Howard Cessna's work from 1935, including commentaries and corrections.

House of Cessna, Book Three: An report of in depth research done in France while searching for the family's origin.

Early Cessna Farms: A meticulous search of deeds to identify the locations of Cessna farms from 1718 through 1810. GPS coordinates provided were possible.

Muster Call: A partial listing of Cessna members of this family who have served in the US Military.

Our Fifteen Minutes:
A collection of humorous, sad and inspiring newspaper articles spotlighting family members in moments of fame and infamy over the past 250 years.

Available on Amazon

INTRODUCTION

In this work, I have tried to reconstruct a form of Family Census; using all of the references we have for individuals in various locations. By merging this data with the two books of Howard Cessna; and Family Trees reported on Ancestry; I try to identify the makeup of the early families.

In most cases, I worked backwards to establish dates and locations of birth. For example: if Charles Cessna is 85 years old in the 1850 Census and was born in Pennsylvania. I know he was born about 1765. By eliminating all of the families which have a known Charles, I could "Guestimate" which household he belongs to.

MISSING CHILDREN:

Among the children of John Cessna II (the patriarch from Shippensburg), only Maj. John, James, Theophilus, Jonathan and Joseph have left clear records of their children's names. Children of their brothers: William, Charles and Evans remain a puzzle to be pieced together. Any descendants of his daughters Mary, Elizabeth and Margaret remain a complete mystery.

In earlier years of my research, I made the assumption that the grandchildren, John and Elizabeth, mentioned in the Will of John II, were William's only children. Yet there were just too many "Johns", "Charles" and "Williams" in Cumberland and Bedford Counties to make sense. This misdirected me to round up all of the unexplained references into a picture of a third brother coming from Ireland. **I now believe I was wrong**.

I have employed **Occum's Razor**....when faced with a mystery, "the simplest explanation is most often the right one."

RULE OF TWENTY-FIVE:

By working the dates backwards, and using the "Rule of 25"; I believe I have accounted for the children of William, Charles and Evans. In doing so I was able to place most of my "extra people" into a sensible family chart. In the Addendum of this work you will find more details on how those assumptions were made.

For the years prior to the first official census, I have noted all references to voting, land warrants, taxes, military, etc. which will help us establish location of family members. This helped indicate their parentage.

The Rule of 25: The early settlers were working with virgin land. It took a full year of labor to clear three acres of timber. It took several years of labor to make the required "improvements" to a property before it was ready to be warranted, surveyed and titled. That is usually the first time it appears in government records.

Therefore, while a young man might possibly marry and produce a child by age 20….it was more than likely that he would be 25 years or older before he could find a piece of land, and develop it to the point it could be surveyed, and pay taxes on it.

COMPUTATION OF AGE:

For computation of age, I have assumed that our ancestors were at least 21 years of age when they signed legal petitions to the government, or as witnesses to a deed. I also assume that a minimum of 18 to 24 months was normal between birth of children.

CHAIN REFERENCE NOTES:

To help you **check my calculations**, I have included Chain Reference Notes. After each person's name will be a key, "12/67". The number before the slash tells you the previous page this person was found on; and the number after the slash telling you what page you will next find that person mentioned. In this way, you may trace their lifetime.

UNCERTAIN NAMES:

When I feel **sure** of a name for a child of an individual…but am *not CERTAIN*…I have noted this by printing them in Italics. These are educated guesses to help us identify where following generations fit into the family tree.

DISCLAIMER

I WASN'T THERE! And these folks didn't leave very good notes for genealogists.

That being said, let me assert that I have done my very best to match up all of the data found in 30 years of research; with the family tree that we know about. Frequently, I have had to calculate backwards.

If a Cessna and their family suddenly show up in 1820 and the census says that he is 26-45 years old.....I know he had to be present in 1810 or 1800 and possibly 1790 or 1780. So who did he belong to?

Yes, I have made mistakes. Yes, it is incomplete. But like Howard Cessna in 1901; I think it is time I put what I have found into some cohesive order for the next generation to build on.

Do not assume, I got everything right. Use this as a guide or provocation to keep up your own search.

-C. W. "Bill" Cissna

OTHER TRAILS TO FOLLOW:

There was at least a second migration of the Le Sesne/Cesne family about 50 years later. They settled land on Daniel Island across the bay from Charleston, SC. Unlike our migration, these folks were not Huguenot, but Catholic. All of the family remaining in France after 1685 had to be (or had to become) Catholic.

Another group is investigating the possibility of a third brother coming from Ireland, William Cessna. Grace Boerner writes the following to the House of Cessna FB page.

Grace McChesney Boerner writes: *"Chesney too? I descend from William DeCessna/Chesney b. 1694 Ulster, Ireland. I believe his father was Jean/John LeSisney/DeCessna b. 1669 in France (Huguenot) who went to Ireland & fought in the battle of Boyne."*

And from Shari Sisney…

Shari Sisney: *"William Cessna/Chesney. William was born about 1694 in Ireland. He came to Pennsylvania and settled near the Susquehanna River on land north of that of Stephen (2) Cessna. He married and his wife died before 1752. 1 June 1752 he married Esther (Say, Sey) Harris, the widow of John Harris, at Paxtang Church, now in Harrisburg. Esther and John's son, John Harris, founded the city of Harrisburg. Esther was born in Yorkshire, England and met John Harris, Sr. when she was visiting Shippen relatives in Philadelphia. John Harris, Sr.'s will was signed 22 November 1746 and he died that year.*

"William chose his land wisely along the Susquehanna River, north of Stephen (2)'s land. It was in a good spot for a ferry and he operated one for a number of years. The family became very wealthy and the ferry business contributed greatly to it."

CONTENTS

1718 Newcastle County
At that time Pennsylvania, but became Delaware.

The Cessna brothers arrived by ship from Northern Ireland.

Stephen Cessna/Sisney, born Ireland ca 1693

John Cessna, born in Ireland ca 1699

William Cessna/Chesney (possibly), bn 1695

*As of yet we have found no evidence of Jean de Cesna, the father of these brothers having arrived in this country. Nor have we located his residence in Ireland.

Throughout this book, when providing the ancestry of a person, I will only say the "Frenchman" in defference to Jean de Cessna. And I have used the lesser sign "<" to indicate "the son of".

i.e.: William Cissna<John<John<the Frenchman

1720 CENSUS
Newcastle County, PA
Became Delaware
Area along Brandywine Creek north of
Wilmington

Stephen Cessna/Sisney, bn ca 1695 in Ireland   15/19
     Patience ?-Cessna, bn ca 1700   /19
     John Cessna, bn ca 1720 (will die in 1751)   /19

John Cessna, bn ca 1699 in Ireland   15/19
     (His first child will be born in 1726)

> **Notes:** Family tradition holds that Jean de Cessna, a French Huguenot, and refugee from religious oppression in both France and Ireland came to America with his sons. Congressman John Cessna stated that they arrived in 1718. In 1718 there was a large migration from Northern Ireland of Scotch, Irish and Huguenots; all of whom had been recruited by William Penn.
>
> These people would have landed at Newcastle, PA in "the Lower Counties" which later become Delaware. By 1710, the landing fees in Philadelphia were so expensive that many ship captains began to unload their passengers and cargo at New Castle. From there they would have traveled overland the rest of the way into Philladelphia. Some moved north as new lands became available. Those who were indentured to pay for their passage would have been auctioned or sold on the docks at New Castle.
>
> It would appear from the dates of their children, that the two bothers married within their first few years in Pennsylvania (discouraging but not eliminating any thought that they were indentured to pay for their voyage.)
>
> The names and locations have been extrapolated from information recorded in the 1730's through 1760's.

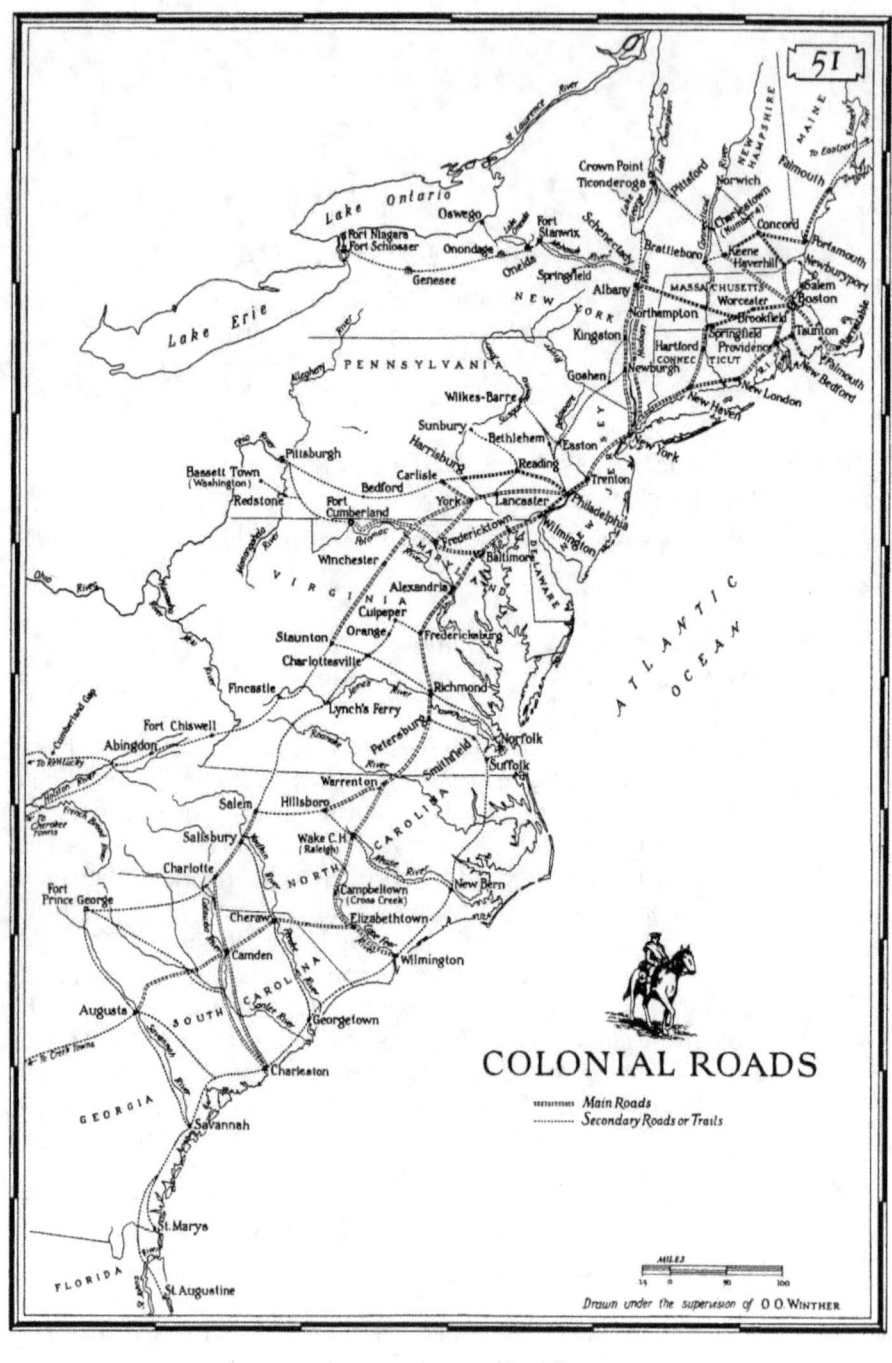

COLONIAL ROADS

▬▬▬▬▬ Main Roads
--------- Secondary Roads or Trails

Drawn under the supervision of O. O. Winther

1730 CENSUS

Newcastle County, PA
Christiana Township

Stephen Cessna, bn ca 1695 in Ireland	17/21
Patience Cessna, ca 1700	17/21
John Cessna, bn ca 1720	17/21
Stephen Cessna Jr, bn ca 1722	/21
Thomas Cessna, bn ca 1728	/21
Theophilus Cessna, bn ca 1730	/21

2 Dec 1738. Richard Nicholas of Christiana Hun. In the County of Newcastle, a carpenter, and Ann his wife, for the sum of £53, sold unto Nicholas Bishop of Mill Creek Hun. In said County, a lott of land situate in Willingtown (sic). It bounds lott of James Millner Junr. On Second St. and contains 11 perches 3 feet. This is the property that Dr. James Millner was seized of by conveyance dated 3 July 1732 (Book K/pp234). Sd Millner by his indenture dated 27 Oct 1736, sold lotts unto his son, Thomas Millner. Then sd Thomas by indenture dated 10 June 1737, sold a lott unto **Stephen Cissna**; then sd Cissna and **Patience** his wife, sold sd lott unto afsd Richard Nicholas. Signed: Richard Nicholas, Ann Nicholas. Wit: **Stephen Cessna**, Neille Fearon. Rec: 13 March 1738. **(This a town lot in Wilmington)** **Note:** Townships were once referred to as "Hun." or Hundred, meaning an area of 100 square miles. Stephen Cissna the sold property, but Stephen Cessna was the witness.

John Cessna, bn ca 1699 in Ireland	17/22
1st Wife of John Cessna, bn ca 1700	
John Cessna Jr, bn 26 Jan 1726	/22
Mary Cessna, bn ca 1730	/22

4 Sept 1738, John Cessna, Joseph Simpson, John Stalop witnessed sale of land by John & Rebecca Day to Nathan Hussey. Tract of land near Brandywine Creek, formerly owned by Andrew Neal.

1738, John Cessna bought a license to settle on land from Bunston's Purchases. See his will and listing for 1740.

1727, John's 1st wife must have died shortly after the birth of their son, John, in 1726. He remarried about 1740.

Observation: During the first two generations daughters were surely born; yet only the names of daughters of John Cessna in Shippensburg have been preserved for us. Any daughters of Stephen and Patience would appear in later records under their married names, and be difficult to identify.

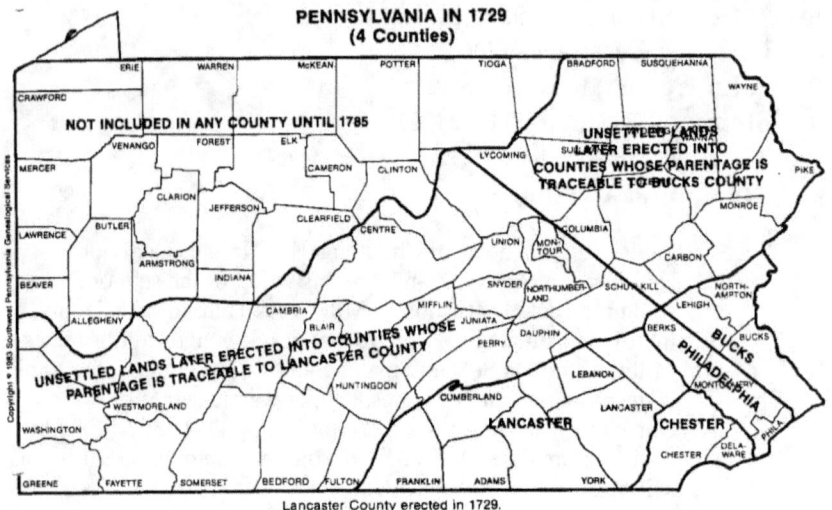

Lancaster County erected in 1729.

1740-45 Census

1740 Lancaster County, PA
At a plantation along the Swatara Creek
at a point called Pine Ford;
near the Susquehanna River.

Stephen Cessna/Sisney, bn ca 1695 in Ireland   19/25
    Patience Sisney, bn ca 1700   19/25
    John Cessna, bn ca 1720 (married Priscilla Foulke ca 1744)   19/25
    Thomas Cessna, bn ca 1726   19/26
    Theophilus Cessna/Cisney, bn ca 1730   19/25

1740, Sheriff's sale for land southeast of Swatara creek at the
    Susquehanna on Messuage Plantation, land described as late in
    the occupation of Stephen Foulke and taken on execution at the
    suit of Stephen Cessnay.
1 July 1741, John Smooze of Lancaster County sold 53 acres in Leacock
    Twp. and Stephen Cessna signed as a witness.
November 1741, Stephen Sesney was a member of the grand jury for
    Lancaster County.
17 October 1743, Stephen Cessney had 200 acres surveyed and titled in
    Lancaster County. Land warrant was issued at Shippensburg to
    Stephen Cessna Sr, for a plantation that had been surveyed for
    Mr. Campbell in 1740.
17 October 1743, warrants of Lancaster County, #217 (Stephen Cessney)
    and #369 (Stephen Sissing, via patentee Michael Grove,
    warranted for 300 acres and 150 acres respectively in
    Derry Township. Record states that Cessna first applied for
    Warrant and the request was returned. Later, Michael Grove
    applied for a Patent on this land that Cessna had surveyed.
1744, Quarter Sessions Court of Lancaster County; a number of people
    petition or a new road to Lancaster from Harris's Ferry. Road
    would cross the Swatara Creek at Stephen Sisner's plantation.
    Stephen and John Cessna both sign.
About 1744, The son of Stephen and Patience, John Cessna, married
    Priscilla Foulke and moved over the Susquehanna River to what
    will be Newberry Twp in York County. Their son Stephen was
    born ca 1745.

1740 Lancaster County
"Over the Susquehanna"
Probably land on Conodoguinet Creek NW of Shippensburg.

John Cessna, bn 1699 in Ireland	19/26
Unknown 2nd wife, bn ca 1720	19/26
John Cessna, bn 1726	19/26
Mary Cessna, bn ca 1727-30	/26
William Cessna, born 1741	/26
Margaret Cessna, born 1743	/26
Charles Cessna, born 1744 or 26-30	/26
Joseph Cessna, born 1747	/26
Elizabeth Cessna, bn ca 1745	19/26

In the 1730's. the Penns gave Samuel Blunston authority to issue land deeds in the form of Licenses. They were promissory notes to issue a proper deed whenever they were able to do so legally. John Casney is recorded on page 7 as a purchaser. In his Will of 1793, John describes this land as: "Also a grant of land got from Mr. Blunston's, lying near the Susquehanna River, on the west side in York County, near Conewago Creek, and adjoining the same about a mile west from the River joining on the Branch of Dry Inlet." Other Bluston Licenses were issued for land where present day Carlisle and Shippensburg are located. About 1750-51, John purchased several of these from those first given Blunston licenses. In his will, John states that he never developed this land.

Warrant #29, John Cassen, requested survey for 200 acres on west Side of Susquehanna River dated 26 Oct 1737. Returned 10 0ct 1822 and patented for 211.98 acres by Henry Longsdorf. Recorded Vol H #19, p 232. Also, 55 acres of this warrant was returned 3 Mar 1870 and patented by Noah Seits & John Martin. Recorded Patent Book Vol H #65, p 476.

The first farm west of the Susquehanne that was actually settled and lived on by John Cessna appears to be a farm on Conodoquinet Creek. 16 Dec 1755, John Cessna was granted a Warrant by the Proprietaries of Pennsylvania for a 277 ¾ acre farm on Conodoquinet Creek. It is evident that he had settled on this farm years earlier because he is on the tax roll of 1751-51.

1740 Philadelphia City

Stephen Cessna Jr, <Stephen Cessna/Sisney<The Frenchman   19/26

26 April 1748, John French recorded in his will that his sole beneficiary is Stephen Cessna a resident of Philadelphia; "my true and loving friend." Stephen appears to have left Philadelphia after this and moved to be near his parents in Carlisle, Cumberland County.

1750-55 Census

Pennsylvania

1750 Cumberland County, PA

On January 27, 1750; the Pennsylvania Assembly created Cumberland County out of Lancaster County. Until then this region had been known as "Lancaster Over the Susquehanna." In the late 1740's Penn began to buy out the Scotch-Irish settlers East of the Susquehanna and move them to the West side of the River. This was in response to complaints from the Quaker Brethren that the Scotch and Irish were unruly neighbors. It was felt that their quarreling nature would make them a good buffer between the Quakers and the Indians living to the West.

License was given to settle and improve wilderness land. But the land was not usually surveyed and deeded until several years later, when substantial improvements had been made (fields cleared, barns and house erected, etc). It was at that point that a payment was made to pay the government. In 1754, after the Albany Purchase, that title to land in Cumberland County could be purchased.

1750 Carlisle, PA

Stephen Sisney/Cessna, bn ca 1695 in Ireland   21/
    Patience ?-Sisney, bn ca 1700   21/28
    Theophilus Sisney, bn ca 1730   21/28

1751, Cumberland County Tax, Stephen Cesna, West Pennsborough Twp (Carlisle).

16 March 1754, Stephen Cesna of Cumberland Co., yeoman, & Patience his wife, made a mortgage of 20£ to William Dillwood for the home on lot #187 of Carlisle. Note due 1 Oct 1754.

April 1756, Court Records state that Stephen Sisney "is sick and in jail at the suit of Daniel Hogen." Sisney stated that it "is an unjust debt regarding a hat."

5 Oct 1757, Stephen was still in jail and severely ill. The court issued administration to Arther Foster and Patience Cessna.

18 April 1758, Property of Stephen Sesna, deceased, was sheriff-ed and sold to William Russel, a perry-wigmaker.

5 May 1762, William Russell of Carlisle, a barber, sold lot #187 to Thomas Porter of the town of York, York County, PA, a tabocconist, for 92£ 10 shillings.

Stephen Sisney Jr, bn ca 1724   23/

(There is no indication that he ever married)

31 August 1756 Stephen Sisna died, His estate was inventoried on 18 April 1763, by appraisers Boggs and Piper: 1 cow.. £2.15; 1 Chest.. 5 sh; 1 small box… 2 sh. 6 p; To putter… £1. 5 sh; 1 small tea kettle…0; To one old bed…3 sh; a small pot...2sh 6p. Total: £7. 9 sh. This must be a son of Stephen and Patience because he was an adult, and evidently single. Stephen, husband of Patience, was still living, but in jail on 31 Aug 1756.

Thomas Sisney, bn ca 1726   21/26
  Margaret Gallacher-Sisney, bn ca 1730   21/26
  Stephen Cissna, *will be born 1755*   /26

15 Sep 1755, baptism in Carlisle of Stephen Sisney, son of Thomas and Margaret Sisney.

1750 Shippensburg, PA

John Cessna, bn ca 1699 in Ireland	22/32
2nd wife, bn ca 1720	22/32
John Cessna, bn 26 Jan 1726	22/35
William Cessna, bn 1741	22/33
Margaret Cessna, born 1743 (married Robert Hall ca 1761)	/32
Charles Cessna, bn 2 Mar 1744	22/33
Elizabeth Cessna, bn ca 1745 (married Thomas Jones ca 1762)	/34
Joseph Cessna, bn 1747	22/36
Jonathan Cessna, bn ca 1749	/36

James Cessna, *will be born 1751*   /27
Evans Cessna,   /34
1737, Edward Shippen purchased two tracts of land that would become
      Shippensburg in January and March of 1737; a total of 1312
      Acres. John Cessna was listed one of the first occupants of
      Shippensburg, having rented from Edward Shippen.
1751, Cumberland County Tax, John Cesna, Lurgan Twp.
1753, Cumberland County Tax, John Cesna, Lurgan Twp.
July 1754, a petition was delivered to the Pennsylvania Assembly,
      requesting government to provide protection for citizens from
      Indians and other marauders. Among the signatories is John
      Cesna of Shippensburg.
8 July 1755, John Sisney warranted 25 acres in Cumberland County.
18 July 1757, John Cessna and sons Joseph & Jonathan are kidnapped
      from their harvest field near Shippensburg.

The Conodoquinet Creek Farm
rented by Andrew Neal from John Cessna

Mr. Neale
Mary Cessna-Neale bn ca 1730   18/32

1771 The Cumberland County Court ordered a road to be built from
      Shippensburg to Cesna's Gap. It will pass through what is now
      Orrstown, past a farm that is owned by John Cessna, previously
      the home of Andrew Neal.

1750 York County, PA

John Cessna, bn ca 1720   17/
Pryscilla Foulke-Cessna, bn ca 1725   /35
Stephen Cessna/Sisney, bn ca 1745   /35
John Cessna/Sisney, bn ca 1747   /35
Ruth Cessna/Sisney, bn ca 1748   /35

1749, John Cesna attended a wedding at the Quaker Warrington Monthly
      Meeting. He was not a Quaker but listed as a guest.
1747, List of Officers of the Associated Regiment of Lancaster County,
      over the river Susquehanna shows Ensign John Cesna.
30 April 1751, Inhabitants near Yellow Breeches Creek in the County of
      York petitioned for a road to be built to George Groghon's
      place towards Harris Ferry, beginning at Yellow Breeches Creek
      at Cesney Ford.
22 July 1751, "Return for a road from Sessney's Fording" toward Georg
      Croghan….begins at Cesney Fording on Yellow Breeches

Creek, below James Fraizers Mill….then north toward Samuel Jones Plantation….northeast to George Thawley's Plantation ….then northwest to George Croghan on the above creek…from Fraziers Mill to Harris' Ferry."

6 Aug 1751, Will of John Cessna, a Skin-dresser, in Newberry twp, York County. Left possessions (but no land) to wife Priscilla and children: Stephen, John and Ruth.

1750 Cumberland Valley Twp Bedford

(along the road from Raystown to Fort Cumberland)

No Cessna's yet.

Cumberland County was first settled by a majority of Scots-Irish immigrants who arrived in this area about 1730. English and German settlers constituted about ten percent of the early population. The settlers originally mostly devoted the area to farming and later developed other trades.   These settlers built the Middle Spring Presbyterian Church among the oldest houses of worship in central Pennsylvania, in 1738 near present-day Shippensburg, Pennsylvania.

27 Jan 1750, The General Assembly (legislature) of the Pennsylvania Colony created Cumberland County, naming it for Cumberland, England. The County seat was Shippensburg, but quickly moved to Carlisle. The county also lies within the Cumberland Valley adjoining the Susquehanna River at its eastern border, stretching about 42 miles from the borough of Shippensburg on the west to the Susquehanna River in east Cumberland County.

By 1750 Raystown (Bedford) was a well known post on the trader's path. The people who settled there were farmers and considered a menace by the Delawares and Shawnee, who regarded the Juniata Valley as their richest hunting ground. After repeated complaints by the Indians through the Iroquois, Pennsylvania authorities ordered the magistrate of Cumberland County to evict them and burn their cabins in May of 1750. But the settlers were not arrested and promptly returned to rebuild.

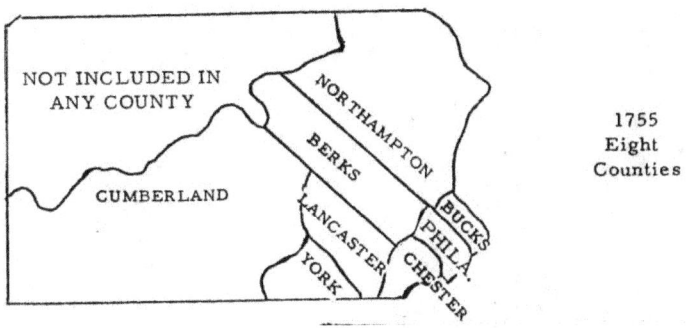

NOT INCLUDED IN
ANY COUNTY

NORTHAMPTON

BERKS

CUMBERLAND

LANCASTER

BUCKS

PHILA.

YORK

CHESTER

1755
Eight
Counties

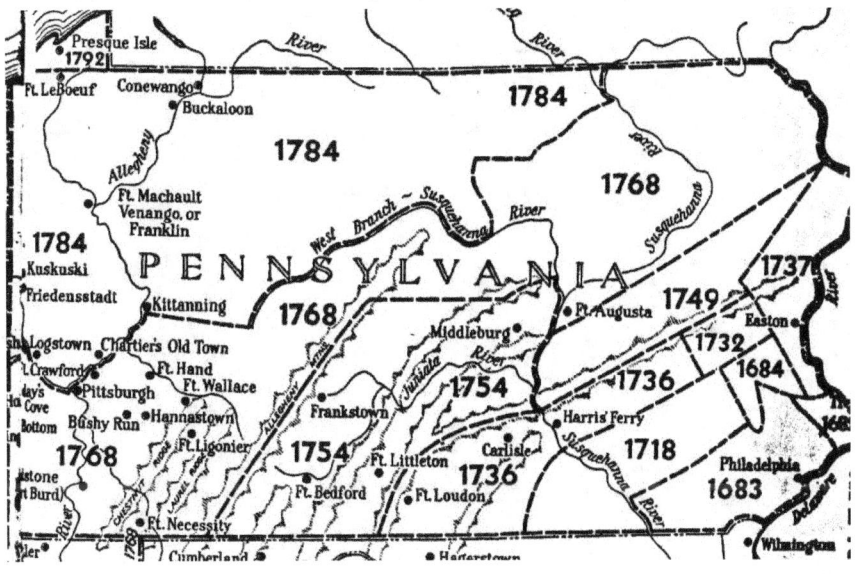

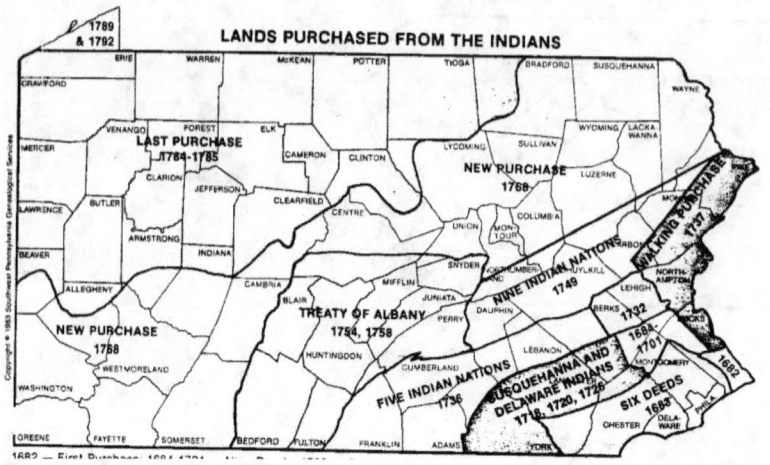

1760 Census
Pennsylvania

1760 Cumberland County, PA
Carlisle

Thomas Sisney, bn ca 1726 <Stephen>the Frenchman   21/
   Margaret Gallacher-Sisney, bn ca 1730   21/
   Stephen Sisney/Cissna, bn 1755   21/39

> 30 Nov 1763, James Hamilton married Margreth Cisney, alias
> Gallacher. Hamilton married again 3 years later. So Thomas
> died before 1763 and Margaret died ca 1765. Note that Patience
> left Carlisle after her husband's death in 1758. Stephen joined
> Grandmother Patience after his mother's death.

1760 West of Shippensburg

Big Cove Farm
Patience Sisney, bn ca 1700, Widow of Stephen<Frenchman   25/43
   Theophilus Cissna, bn ca 1730 <Stephen>the Frenchman   25/43
   Sarah Cissna, wife of Theophilus married ca 1760   /43
   Stephen Cissna, bn 1755 <Thomas<Stephen<Frenchman   26/43

Patience moved from Carlisle after their home and property was sold. She
took up a homestead 15 miles West of Shippensburg; and sold this claim
in March 1763 . Following the French & Indian War there were hundreds
of abandoned farms in Cumberland County. They were available for
homesteading with little or no money.

> In 1761, Widow Sisney, a neighbor of Charles Stewart and William
> Maxwell in Aire Twp paid tax on 150 acres, unwarranted.
> 15 March 1763, David Stewart applied for a warrant on 100 acres of land,
> called "the improvements of Patience Cessna" on Big Cove
> (creek), next to land of Charles Stewart and William Maxwell in
> Aire Twp. (later to become Fulton County.)

25 Aug 1763, Patience Sisney petitioned Cumberland County orphan's court to appoint Wm. Smith as guardian for her grandsons; Stephen and John Sisney (sons of John Sisney, deceased) and Stephen Sisney (son of Thomas, deceased). Court was held in Shippensburg (not Carlisle) to settle estates of those killed during the war.

1760 Lurgan Twp.
Farm on Conondoguinet Creek

Mr. Neale
      Mary Cessna-Neale bn ca 1730   27/
      Probable Children

1760 Shippensburg

John Cessna, bn ca 1699 in Ireland	26/42
Unnamed wife, bn ca 1720	26/42
Evans Cessna, bn 1750	26/42
James Cessna, bn 1751	26/42
Margaret Cessna, bn ca 1756	26/33
Elizabeth Cessna, bn ca 1750	26/35
Theophilus Cessna, bn 1760	/42

3 June 1762, John Chisney bought 50 acres in Cumberland County
4 Sep 1767, John Cessna & William Campbell, bought 200 acres, 1 mile
      east of Shippensburg (mentioned in John's will).
8 Sep 1755, John Sisney, bought 25 acres Cumberland County,
16 Dec 1756, John Sisney, bought 100 acres.
1762 Cumberland County, Tax, John Sisner, Hopewell twp.
1764 Cumberland Cty Tax, John Sisner, East Pennsborough twp,
      100 acres.
1764 Cumberland Cty Tax, John Cisney, Hopewell Twp, 1 lot.

Robert Hall   Married 1760-63
Margaret Cessna, born 1743   /26

24 Mar 1763, Robert Hall of Lurgan Twp purchased a tract of land in
      Cumberland Valley from William Coulter.
17 May 1763, Robert Hall and Evans Cessna applied for a Warrant (and
      survey) on 350 acres; including the improvements of Phillip
      Baltimore and Thomas Jones.

19 Jul 1768, Robert Hall of Lurgan Twp sold his half interest to John
   Cessna Sr of Hopewell Twp, for 40£. This sale was witnessed
   by Joseph Cissna and Evan Cissna. A later deed states Hall sold
   it to Cessna for a debt, and that he was still residing in Lurgan
   Twp.

1760 Letterkenny Twp.
Will become Franklin County

William Cessna, bn 1741   <John<Frenchman   26/43
   Margaret Williamson   /44
   William W. Cessna, bn 1760 <William<John<Frenchman   /44
   Charles Cessna, bn ca 1761 <William<John<Frenchman   /44
   John Cessna, bn ca 1765 <William<John<Frenchman   /44

1763 Cumberland Cty tax, Charles Cissney, Letterkenny twp. No land,
   just personal property.
1763 Cumberland Cty Tax, John Cissney, Letterkenny twp, 50 acres.
1764 Cumberland Cty Tax, John Cisney, Letterkenny twp, 100 acres.
1793, John Cessna sold this farm to William and Margaret Cessna, who
   immediately sold it. John held tittle until he was ready to write
   his will.

THESE TOWNSHIPS WILL BECOME BEDFORD COUNTY

Cumberland Valley Twp
about 1763

Charles Cessna, bn 2 Mar 1744   <John<the Frenchman   26/37
   Elizabeth Culbertson   /37
   John Cessna, bn ca 1763   /37
   Samuel Cessna, bn ca 1765   /37

3 June 1763 Charles Cessna applied for a Warrant of 100 acres in
   Cumberland County. Land was next to John Cessna Jr. Warrant

cost 9£. Annual Quit Rents were 4sh 2p. Deed stated that the land was known as Ackney's Bottoms.

2 Aug 1766, Daniel Duncan applied for Warrant of 100 acres near John Casnay Jr and Charles Casnay in Cumberland Valley.

23 Nov 1766, James Levinston of Patrick County Maryland sold to Charles Cessna for 150£, a certain tract of land in Cumberland ValleyTwp; joining on the north, a tract of land belonging to Jonathan Cessna. 23 Nov 1766 was date of sale. But it was not recorded until 23 May 1797. Charles named the plantation "Reliance".

30 Aug 1768, James Culbertson, applied for Warrant of 200 acres, next to Charles Cessna.

Taxes for Cumberland County/Bedford County
> 1767 Cumberland Valley Twp Cumberland County, Charles Sisney, 200 acr warranted, 10 cleared, 2 horses, 2 cows
> 1768 Cumberland Valley Twp Cumberland County, Charles Cesney, 150 acr warranted, 11 cleared, 2 horses, 2 cows.

Note: Charles' son, John appears once in Bedford Militia records. John and Samuel appear with Charles in Georgia records.

Thomas Jones   Married 1760-63
Elizabeth Cessna-Jones, bn ca 1750   <John<Frenchman   26/
(Elizabeth died childless)

20 Feb 1767, Jonathan Cessna signed as a witness for sale of Cumberland Valley twp land by James Levingston of Frederick County, MD to Thomas Jones.

17 May 1763, Thomas Jones & Charles Cessna of the county of Cumberland warrant 300 acres, including improvements, adjoining Robert Hall and Evan Cessna, on the branch of Evitts Creek.

11 Jul 1767, Thomas Jones sold his half to Samuel Purviance after his wife died.

Evans Cessna   27/39
Mary ?-Cessna
Thomas Cessna bn ca 1765

24 Mar 1763, Robert Hall of Lurgan Twp purchased a tract of land in Cumberland Valley from William Coulter.

17 May 1763, Robert Hall and Evans Cessna applied for a Warrant (and survey) on 350 acres; including the improvements of Phillip Baltimore and Thomas Jones.

19 Jul 1768, Robert Hall of Lurgan Twp sold his half interest to John
Cessna Sr of Hopewell Twp, for 40£. This sale was witnessed
by Joseph Cissna and Evan Cissna. A later deed states Hall sold
it to Cessna as payment of a debt.

1760 Colerain Twp.

John Cessna (Jr?), bn 1726   <John<the Frenchman   26/35
    Sarah Rose-Cessna, bn ca 1740   /35
    Jonathan Cessna, bn 16 Nov 1760   /35

1 Aug 1766, Early land warrant application; John Cessna:150 acres,
including his improvements next to John Cessna Jr., in
Cumberland Valley, 10 miles from Bedford.
3 Jun 1762, Cumberland Co tax: John Chisney, 150 a.
4 Mar 1766, Samuel Finley bought 200 acres from John Cesna Jr,
adjoining land of Charles Cessna, the improvements of William
Kirkpatrick, & land of Wm Trent, known by the name of The
Block Houses on both sides of Evitts Creek in Cumberland Co.
2 Aug 1766, Daniel Duncan, 100 acres near John Casnay Jr and
Charles Casney in Cumberland Valley.
1767, Charles Sisney, paid tax in Bedford County
1767, Landowners for Bedford County: John Sisney, Jr, Adam Sisney,
John Sisney, Sr., Charles Sisney. Note: Adam is probably Evan.
2 Aug 1768, Daniel Duncan bought 100 acres in Cumberland Valley
Twp, near land owned by John Cessna, Jr and Charles Cessna.
30 Aug 1768, James Culbertson, 200 acres, next to Charles Cessna.

1760 York County, PA

Pryscilla Foulke-Cessna, bn ca 1725   27/37
    Widow of John<Stephen<Frenchman
    Stephen Cessna/Sisney, bn ca 1745   27/37
    John Cessna/Sisney, bn ca 1747   27/37
    Ruth Cessna/Sisney, bn ca 1748   27/

9 Jul 1763, Stephen, John and Ruth Sisney, step-children of Abraham
Elliott are received at a meeting in Warrington Quaker Meeting.
(In 1764, Abraham Elliott will move this family to Orange
County, North Carolina).
1 Feb 1766 Ruth Cessna/Sisney married Wm Beason in NC. She died
13 Nov 1768.

French Canada

1760 Pottawatomie Village near Detroit
(River Rouge area)

Joseph Cessna, bn 1747   <John<the Frenchman   26/34
    (captive of Pottawatomie from 1757-1762)

Jonathan Cessna, bn 1749   <John<the Frenchman   26/38
    (captive of Pottawatomie from 1757-1762)

    This is per the story told in the obituary of Joseph Glass Cissna,
            grandson of Joseph.
    18 Jul 1757, A list of those killed and missing at John Cisney's field
            about 7 miles from Shippensburg: Killed were John Kirkpatrick,
            Dennis O'Neidon. Missing, Cisney and three small boys; two
            sons of Cisney and one son of Kirkpatrick.
    "The Papers of Henry Bouquet", Pennsylvania Historical and   Museum
            Commission, volume 5, page 822. Bouquet to Burd at Fort Pitt
            13th October 1761. Coll Bouquet's Compliments to Col. Burd,
            have received his note from Fort Detroit, in regard to the two
            sons of John Sisney & one son of Widow Kirkpatrick, & I shall
            take the first opportunity for Detroit to write to Capt Campbell,
            to have them sent here.
    17 May 1762, Jonathan and Joseph Cessna are recorded as buying 300
            acres in Cumberland Valley Twp: land that is in dispute with
            Maryland. This is just after their escape from captivity, and they
            are both underage (12 & 15). Land had been purchased by their
            father in their names shortly after their escape and return.

1770 CENSUS

1770 North Carolina

1770 Guilford County

Abraham Elliott
    Priscilla Foulke-Cessna-Elliott, bn ca 1725   31/
        Widow of John<Stephen<the Frenchman
    John Sisney/Cessna, bn 1747   31/57
        <John<Stephen<the Frenchman

    In 1790 Census John Sisney was listed as Joseph Sisney
    1766, Ruth Sisney, daughter of John, Roan County, NC, married William
        Beeson at New Garden Monthly Meeting in North Carolina.
        Ruth died in childbirth 1768)

Stephen Sisney/Cessna, bn 1745   35/43
        <John<Stephen<the Frenchman
    Dolly Holten-Sisney, bn ca 1660   /43
    John Sisney, bn ca 1769   /43
    Rachel Cisney, bn ca 1770 (married Mr. Taylor)   /43

    1762 Tax in Rowan County, NC   Stephen Sissney
    1768, Stephen Sisney married Dolly Holten. Was ejected from Quaker
        Fellowship for "marrying outside the church."
    5 Sept 1771, Stephen Cesney witnessed a will for William Hoggatt in
        Guilford County, NC.
    23 Sep 1776, Advertisement of Escaped prisoners: Tories who broke Gaol
        at Frederick Town. Stephen Sysney a Pennsylvania 5 feet 5
        inches high, a well portioned man has a dimple on his chin, short
        dark brown hair, a hunting shirt, brown shalloon jackett, leather
        breeches, and a pair of trousers, stockings, shoes and a large hat.
    Note: It seems logical that Stephen and Dolly would have had children
        between 1768 and 1775.

1770 Pennsylvania

1770 Bedford County, PA
(formed from Cumberland County 1771)

Bedford Township

Jonathan Cessna, bn 1749   <John<the Frenchman   36/45
    Mary Friend-Cissna, bn ca 1756   /45
    William Cessna, bn 17 Jun 1776   /45
    Nancy Agnes Cessna, bn ca 1774   /45

20 February 1767, Jonathan Cessna signed as a witness for sale of
    Cumberland Valley twp land by James Levingston of Frederick
    County, MD to Thomas Jones. Jonathan was just 17 yrs old.
1774 Bedford Twp tax, Jonathan Cissna   .11.
1775 Bedford Twp. Tax, Jonathan Sissna   14.10 (14 shillings 10 pence).

1770 Cumberland Valley Township

Col. Charles Cessna, bn 1724   28/53
                <John<the Frenchman
Elizabeth Culbertson Cessna, bn ca 1740   28/53
John Cessna, bn ca 1762
Samuel Cessna, bn ca 1765   28/53
Elizabeth Cessna, bn ca 1767   /53
Unknown bn ca 1764   /54
Mary Cessna, bn ca 1774   /54
Robert Cessna, bn ca 1768   /54

27 Oct 1770, Charles Cessna witnessed to sale of Cumberland Valley twp
    land by Adam McCartney to Bernard Dougherty.
9 Mar 1771, Bedford County was created from part of Cumberland
1771-76, John and Charles Cessna were listed as jurors in Jan courts for
    each of these years.
16 Apr 1771, Charles Cessna served on Grand Jury of Bedford County
    at 1st meeting of Qtr Sessions.
1771 Tax of Cumberland Valley Twp, Cumberland County
    Charles Cesna, 300 acres warranted, 30 cleared, 3 horses, 3 cows

1772, Charles Cessna paid tax in Cumberland Valley twp.

1 Oct 1772, Charles Cessna named Commissioner for Qtr Sessions of Bedford County.

14 Jul 1772, among jurors in Bedford Co was "Charles Cissnay Jr."

17 May 1773; Thos Jones and Charles Cessna apply for 300 acres including improvements adjacent to Evan Cessna and Robt Hall on Branch of Evitts creek, about two miles from the Block Houses.

1 Oct 1773, Charles Cessna was elected commissioner of Bedford County.

16 April 1771, Charles Cessna was recorded as serving on the first Grand Jury in Bedford County, and also the first meeting of the Quarter Sessions Court.

1 Oct 1772, Charles Cessna was named commissioner for Quarter Sessions for Bedford County.

1772 Cumberland Valley Taxables: Charles Cessna, 290 acres

1773   Tax of Cumberland Valley twp, Charles Cessna   5.0

1774   Cumberland Valley twp
  Charles Cessna   5.0 (shillings.pence)
  Charles Cessna   .5

1775   Tax Cumberland Valley twp
  Charles Cessna   19.0
  Charles Cessna   14.5

1776   Tax Cumberland Valley twp
  Charles Cessna   10.10   uncultivated land 16.10

24 Dec 1774, Charles Cessna was elected commissioner of Bedford County.

Jul 1776, Charles Cessna listed as Major in 2nd Battalion of Bedford County, Militia: Col George Woods, commanding.

1777, Charles Cessna listed as Lt. Col in 1st Battalion of Bedford County, Militia

13 Jun 1777, Thomas Urie elected Sheriff. John and Charles Cessna post his surety bond.

30 Oct 1777, in general election, John Cessna elected Sheriff and Charles Cessna elected state rep at PA Assembly.

1778, Tax list of CV twp in Bedford county showed Charles Cessna as owning 290 acr (50 cleared) 1 negro age 20, 1 horse, 2 mares, 4 horned cattle and 6 sheep.

1779, Charles Cessna paid tax on 297 acres 3 horses, 6 cattle, 1 slave; in CV twp.

Capt. Evan Cessna, bn 1728-35 <John<the Frenchman 27/44 & 54
 Mary Cessna, bn ca 1740   27/44 & 54
 Thomas Cessna, bn ca1764   27/44 & 54
 Samuel Cessna, bn ca 1768   /54
 John Cessna, bn ca 1770   /54

1770 Tax Cumberland Valley twp.
     Evan Cesney, 250 acres warranted, 14 cleared, 2 horses, 2 cows
     Thomas Jones, no acres, 4 horses
1771 Tax Cumberland Valley Twp of Cumberland County
     Evans Cesna, 250 acres warranted, 14 cleared, 2 horses, 1 cow
1772 Tax Cumberland Valley : Evan Cessna 200 acres
1773 Tax for Cumberland Valley twp, Evan Cessna   .6
Apr 1773, Evan Cessna appointed Constable in Bedford Co, "sworn in"
     July 1773.
17 May 1773, Thos Jones and Charles Cessna applied for 300 acres
     including improvements adjacent to Evan Cessna and Robt Hall
     on Branch of Evitts creek, about two miles from the block
     houses.
1774   Cumberland Valley twp, Evan Cessna 3.2 (shillings.pence)
     300 acres warranted, 7 cleared, 2 horses, 2 cows
1775   Tax for Cumberland Valley twp, Evan Cessna 15.12
     150 acres, 15 cultivated 85, uncultivated, 2 horses, 2 cows
1776   Cumberland Valley twp, Evan Cessna 5.9: uncultivated land 6.0
1778 Tax of CV twp Evan Cessna, 200 A (15 improved & 10 cleared)
     1 horse, 1 mare, 3 horned cattle, 4 sheep.

Joseph Cesna/Cissna, bn 1747   <John<the Frenchman   31/44

1771 Cumberland Valley Twp of Cumberland County
     Joseph Cesna, 250 acres warranted, 13 cleared, 2 horses, 2 cows
Note: Joseph paid tax on this land, but it appears he has already relocated
to Mt. Pleasant Twp, just west of Fort Pitt.

John Cessna of Shippensburg and **John Cessna Jr** bought several
farms in Cumberland Valley Twp; but lived in Shippensburg and
Colerain Valley Twp respectively.

1766, From applications or land on West side of the Susquehanna: case
     #517, John Cisny, on Evitts Creek, Cumberland Valley Twp,
     Bedford County, 150 acres "including his improvement"
     adjoining lands of John Cessna in Cumberland Valley between
     said Cisny's land and Bedford, about 10 miles from Bedford.
1771 Tax Cumberland Valley Twp of Cumberland County
     John Cesna Jr, 200 acres warranted, 12 acres clear
1772 Tax Cumberland Valley John Cessna, 250 acres
1773 Tax for Cumberland Valley twp, John Cessna
1773 Tax of Cumberland Valley twp, John Cessna, 6 pence
1774 Tax Cumberland Valley twp, John Cessna , 5 pence
1775 Tax Cumberland Valley twp, John Cessna, 10.7 (sh.pence)

1776 Tax Cumberland Valley twp John Cessna, uncultivated land 11.3 no provincial tax

1779 Tax Cumberland Valley twp, John Cessna Sr,100 acres, no animals

2 Aug 1766, Daniel Duncan, 100 acres near John Casnay Jr and Charles Casney in Cumberland Valley.

1767, Land owners for Bedford County: John Sisney, Jr, Adam Sisney (probably Evan), John Sisney, Sr., Charles Sisney

2 Aug 1768, Daniel Duncan bought 100 acres of land in Cumberland Valley Twp, near land owned by John Cessna, Jr and Charles Cessna.

Jan 1775, Court Sessions: King Vs Edward Higgins, he is bound for 100 lbs, Thomas Jones and John Cessna bound for 50£ to keep peace for 1 yr with Daniel Stoy.

1778, Tax list of CV twp John Cessna, 300 A (20 cleared).

30 Oct 1777, in general election, John Cessna elected Sheriff and Charles Cessna elected state rep at PA Assembly.

1770 Colerain Township
Farm near Rainsburg

John Cessna (Maj John), bn 1726 <John<the Frenchman		30/45
Sarah Rose-Cessna, bn ca 1740		30/45
Jonathan Cessna Sr, bn 16 Nov 1760		30/49
Rachel Cessna, bn 1 Aug 1762		/45
John Cessna Jr, bn 8 Dec 1764		/45
Stephen Cessna/Cisna, bn 28 Dec 1766		/45
Elizabeth Cessna, bn 1 Dec 1768		/45
William Cessna Esq will be born 20 June 1775		/45

1774 Colerain Twp tax, John Cessna,   6 shillings .5 pence
1775 Colerain Twp tax, John Cessna,   13.9
1776 Colerain Twp tax, John Cessna,   12.1
18 Sep 1776, John Cessna is Bedford County Rep to State Constitution Convention, and signed first PA Constitution.

1770 Mt. Pleasant Twp.
(Will become Westmoreland County, then Allegheny)

Joseph Cissna, bn 1747 <John<the Frenchman   32/44
    Wife (possibly Sarah Donnellson)   /44
    William Cissna, bn 1773   /44

    1773 Tax Mt. Pleasant twp, Joseph Cessna   1.0 (Inmate)
    1773, Joseph will marry
    18 May 1775, Joseph Cisna and William Donnellson being bound over
        by the Court of Augusta County, VA (Pittsburgh area) on the
        complaint of Thomas Russell for forcable entry and detainer.
        No persons appearing it was ordered dismissed.

1770 Cumberland County, PA

1770 Lot #17, Shippensburg
NW corner of King and Queen Streets

John Cessna, bn 1699 in Ireland <Frenchman   32/58
    Unnamed 2nd wife   bn ca 1720   32/
    James Cessna, bn 1751 (James married ca 1775)   32/58
    Theophilus Cisney, bn 1760   32/58
    Seven Slaves: Will, Rachael, Pomp, Hannah, Cable,
        Tina, and Gregory.

    1768 & 1779 Hopewell Twp Tax; John Sisney/Cesna
    1768 tax Hopewell Twp Cumberland County
        John Cesney 2 Lots, 1 horse, 1 cow, 6 Sheep, 1 Negro
    1769 tax Hopewell Twp Cumberland County
        John Sisney, 1 lott, 1 negro, 2 horses, 1 cow, 9 sheep
    1770, John Cessna one story Stone House/Store on lot #17 burned down
    1776 Hopewell Twp Cumberland County John Cissna,   2 Negroes,
        2 horses, 2 cows, 3 sheep,   10£ 3 Sh
    1778 First State Tax: Hopewell Twp
        John Cisney, 2 negroes; 0 horses; 1 cow; 2 sheep, 3£ 6 Sh 8 p
    1779 Hopewell Tax   John Sisney   4 horses, $182   3 cows, $32
        2 negroes $330 (Children listed below would have been born
        free according to new Constitution of PA)

1 Lot, $500, total $1800

"Names and Age of my negurs, 27 Oct 1780. Will, age 30; Rachael, age 32; Pomp; Hanna, going on "Toon"; Cayboll, (Cabel) going on four; Gregory going on five; Tina, nine months two weeks old, Those with the boro", signed by James Cessna and John Cessna

1790 Census of Shippensburg: Thomas Neal, 1 male over 16, 4 females
Possible husband of Margaret Cessna.

1770 Lurgan Twp

Part which will become Franklin County

Theophilus Cisna, bn ca 1730 <Stephen<the Frenchman	31/57
Sarah Cissna, bn ca 1740	31/57
Thomas Cisna, bn ca 1760	/57
William Cisna, bn ca 1764	/57
Stephen Cisna, bn ca 1766	/57
James Cisna, bn ca 1770	/57
Stephen Cissna, bn 1755 <Thomas<Stephen<Frenchman	27/58
(Theophilus' orphaned nephew)	
Patience Cessna/Sisney, (Theophilus' mother)	27/

Following the death of his father, Stephen Sisney, in jail in Carlisle during the winter of 1758; Theophilus Cessna/Cesna/Cissna settled a small farm near what would become Fannettsburg, PA. It was a few miles west of Shippensburg. In the 1790's, Theophilus moved to Pittsburgh where he opened a tailoring business. He is listed in the 1800 Census of Pittsburgh as a Blue Dyer (blue being a popular but expensive color for clothing.)

1779 Lurgan Twp Cumberland County
        Theophilus Cessna   70 acres $150
                1 horse $30
                1 Cow $9 $189 total
1779 Theophilas Cessna is pvt 4th in Cpt John Campbell's Co of 1st
        Battn Cumberland County, Lurgan Twp
19 July 1779. Theophelus Cesna called to court to give evidence "to what
        he heard Mary Morrison say, in a threatening manner against
        Henry Scott, what she said she would do to him by day or by
        night."

1770 Letterkenny Twp.

William Cessna, bn 1741   John<the Frenchman   33/55
     Margaret Williamson   33/55
     William W. Cessna, bn 1760   33/51
     Charles Cessna, bn ca 1762   33/59
     John Cessna, bn ca 1770   33/55
     Elizabeth Cessna, bn ca 1774   /55

1771 Tax Cumberland Valley Twp of Cumberland County
     William Cesna, 100 acres Located, 3 cleared
1793, John Cessna held title to this farm on Culbertson's Row until just
     before he made out his will, then sold it to Wm and Margaret.
1779 Hopewell twp tax, Charles Sisney,   1 Lot, $100
*Will of his father stateed that William had children: John &
     Elizabeth. Also states that as of October 1793 Elizabeth is not
     yet 21 years, old but John was "of age".
1775 Tax Letterkenny Twp Cumberland County William Cisney
     100 acres warranted; 30 acres clear   2£ 1 Sh 4D
1776 Tax Letterkenny Twp Cumberland County William Cissney
     100 acres patented, 50 cleared 3£; 35 acres valued at 1£ 5p
     1£ 15Sh 1 horse, 2 cows, 2 sheep,   1£ 6Sh 8p
31 July 1777, Wm Cessna is 2nd Lt in 5th Co, 6th Battn, Letterkenny
     twp, Cumberland County, Cpt James Culbertson. Again May 14, 1778
1778 First State Tax: Letterkenny Twp
     William Cesney, 100 acres warranted, 30 cleared,   3 £ 10 Sh
     61 Acres valued at 1£ 5 pence
     1 horse, 1 cow, tax 6.3.0
Note: Date for William W. Jr's birth taken from 1810 Census of
     Mississippi.

New counties: York (1749), Cumberland (1750), Berks (1752), Northampton (1752)

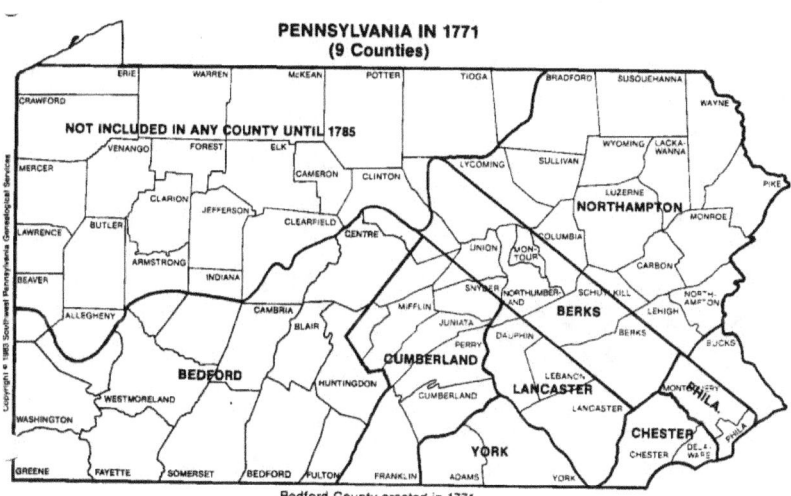

Bedford County erected in 1771.

1780-85 Census

1784 Georgia

1784 Greene County

Col. Charles Cessna, 1784-1790   32/54
     bn ca 1724   <John<the Frenchman
Elizabeth Culbertson-Cessna, bn ca 1743   32/54
Mary Cessna, bn ca 1770 (married Aaron Neel)   32/54
Elizabeth Cessna, bn ca 1772 (married James Milligan)   32/63
Unknown Cessna, bn ca 1768 died b4 1800   32/54
Robert Cessna, bn ca 1768   32/54

Abstracts from Carlisle Gazette: "29 Mar 1786, Sale of Plantation and
     late property of Charles Cessna Esq, in Cumberland Valley, on
     Great Road from Bedford to Cumberland. 300 acres: apply to
     Thomas Coulter, esq near premises; George Funk in Bedford, or
     Thos Smith, James Hamilton or Thos Duncan in Carlisle.
  1787, Thomas Cribbs of Greene County, GA sold to Charles Cessna of
     Greene County, for 35£, 300 acres on waters of Big Beaverdam.
     (land adjoined by Cessna, Reeves, Stewart & Thompson)
10 Aug 1787, John Cesna of Greene County sold to John Lister of Rowan
     Co, NC for 25£, 300 acres of Big Beaverdam Adjoined by
     Robert Christmas.
  1788, Head rights granted to early county residents of Greene County,
     Charles Cessna, 670 acres on Richland Cr.
3 April 1788, Robert Cisney signed a petition asking governor of
     Georgia for permission to raise a company of Horse to defend
     the inhabitants of Greene County.
  1788, Charles Cessna listed as Justice of Peace in Greene County, GA
  1789 Georgia Tax: Greene County/Melton twp, Charles Cesna
1 Aug 1789, Wm Wilson of Green County sold to Robert Maison of
     same county for 65£, 270 ac. on Oakonee River; Part of 670
     acres granted to Charles Cessna on 19 Aug 1788. Witnessed by
     John Cessna & Robert Cessna. (Is Wilson an inlaw?)
  1782, Jonathan Cessna is pvt in Cumberland Valley Twp Militia.
     Note: Jonathan son of Maj. John would have been in the
     Colerain Twp Militia. This might be the unknown son of Col
     Charles.

John Cessna, bn ca 1750   <Charles<John<the Frenchman   34/62
    Mary Cessna, bn ca 1750 wife of John Cessna   34/62
    John Cessna Jr, bn 1770   34/62
    Catherine Cessna, bn ca 1773

1784, John left Bedford County and arrived in Georgia.
1786, John Cessna received land grant in Washington County, GA (land
        was granted first to veterans of Rev War)
31 Dec 1789, John Rice of Green County sold to Moses Shelby for 60£,
        453 acres on Big Beaverdam of Richland Creek, adjoining John
        Cessna.
10 Mar 1789: Lost letters at PO: M. Meals to Merriwether, in file of Jn.
        Cessina
1789 Georgia Tax Digest: Greene County/Melton twp, John Cesna
1786, John Cessna bought 500 acres, Washington County
1788, John Cessna bought 1000 acres, Washington County
Sep 1793, Catherine Cessna was murdered by Indians just outside of
        Greenville, where John Cessna was sheriff.

Samuel Cessna, bn ca 1760   34/56
       <Col. Charles<John<the Frenchman
    Polly Baker-Cessna, bn ca 1766   /56
    Robert Cessna, bn ca 1784   /56
    Elizabeth Cessna, bn ca 1787   /56
    Samuel Cessna Jr, bn ca 1790   /56

1784, Samuel arrived in Georgia.
1784, Head rights granted to early county residents:
        Samuel Sessney, 220 Acres on Richland Creek
1786, Polly Cessna was attacked and scalped. "The first casualty of the
        Indian wars in Greene County was Mrs. Cessna who was
        scalped alive by the Indians while her husband was clearing land
        for planting. She crossed the Oconee river at Cow Ford and
        warned the settlers. These gave pursuit of the savages and killed
        them."
3 April 1788, petition to Govern from inhabitants of Greene County, GA
        asking for a Company of Horse under Captain William Melton
        to defend the frontier. Samuel Cisney signed.
1789 Georgia Tax Digest: Greene County/Melton twp, Samuel Cessna.

1780 North Carolina

1780 Guilford County

Stephen Cessna/Sisney, bn 1745   39/66
        <John<Stephen<the Frenchman
  Dolly Holten-Sisney, bn ca 1759   39/66
  Rachel Cisney, bn ca 1770 (married Mr. Taylor)   39/67
  John Cessna, bn ca 1769   39/66
  Mary Cisney, bn 1783 (married Mr. Grace)   /66
  Elizabeth Cisney, bn ca 1784   /66
  Robert Cisney, bn 1786   /66

1768, Stephen and Dolly were married. He was dis-fellowshiped from the Quaker Church for not following the proper procedures to be married. "Marrying outside the union."

27 Feb 1776, Stephen Sisney was among a company of Torries from Guilford County that was captured. He escaped from prison in Fredricks Town, MD and fought with various groups of Torries in the back country until the war ended in 1781. During that time, Dolly would have lived with her father, Lewis Holton.

Dec 1781, Governor of NC offered pardon for all Torry soldiers who would enlist in Continental Army for 1 year following British Surrender at Yorktown. Stephen is recorded as taking an oath of allegiance and receiving separation pay from Continental Army in Fall of 1782.

William Beason family
  Ruth Beason, daughter of Ruth Cessna Beason, bn 15 May 1767   44/
    <Ruth<John<Stephen<the Frenchman.

1766, Ruth Sisney, daughter of John, Roan County, NC, married William Beeson at New Garden Monthly Meeting in North Carolina. Ruth died in childbirth, 1768)

John Sisney, <Stephen<John<Stephen<the Frenchman
  John Sisney, bn ca 1749   40/63
  Wife of John, bn ca 1755-60   /63

They married ca 1788 and in the 1790 Census have 2 sons.

John Sisney <John<Stephen<Frenchman   /67
Have found no evidence that he is still living at this time.

1780 Pennsylvania

1780 Allegheny County

(part of Westmoreland Cty, that becomes Allegheny, that becomes Washington County)

Joseph Cessna/Cissna, bn 1747   37/65
                 <John Cessna<the Frenchman
      Unnamed Wife, bn ca 1750   1st wife of Joseph   37/
      William Cissna, bn 1773 Mt. Pleasant Twp   37/65
      John Cissna, bn 1775   /65
      James Cissna, bn 1776   /65
      Sarah Cissna bn ca 1779   /65

1774   Cumberland Valley Twp Tax, Joseph Cessna   .5
1775   Cumberland Valley Twp Tax, Joseph Cessna   7.6
1779   Cumberland Valley Twp Tax, Joseph Cesna, 250 acres no animals
1783 Tax/Census Robinson Twp, Washington, County records that
           Joseph Sisney owned 318 acres; has 3 horses; 2 cows; 15
           sheep.
1784, Joseph Cessna was among a large group of people living near
           Pittsburgh who petitoned to move to Detroit area and live under
           British Rule. In testimony he gave at court in Detroit in 1800,
           Joseph states that he moved from Pittsburgh to Detroit in British
           Canada in 1784.
1786 Washington County Tax list: Joseph Cisney
1787 Washington County delinquent tax list: Joseph Cisney

1784 Westmoreland County

Evan Cessna/Cissna,   <John<the Frenchman   35/69
      Mary Cessna, bn 1744   35/69
      Thomas Cessna, bn ca 1764   35/69
      Samuel Cessna, bn ca 1768   35/69
      John Cessna, bn ca 1770   35/69

1785,   Evan Cisney bought lot #223 in Pittsburgh for 13£.
1786   Westmoreland County Tax, Pitt twp, Evan Cesna,   1 sh 6 pence
Note: 1784 Evan moved his family to Pittsburgh at the same time Col.
           Charles and family move to Georgia.

1780 Bedford County

1780 Bedford Twp

Jonathan Cessna, bn 1749   33/
    <John Cessna<the Frenchman
Mary Friend-Cessna, bn ca 1756   33/64
William W. Cessna, bn 17 June 1776   33/64
Agnes Cessna, bn ca 1775   /64

1776, Bedford Twp Tax, Jonathan Sesna   14.01/4 (14£,1 sh, 4P)
25 Mar 1776, Jonathan Cessna is the constable of Bedford Twp.
1779 Bedford twp tax, Jonathan Cesna, 200 acres, 3 horses, 2 cattle
1780, Jonathan joined a large party of settlers, mostly in-laws, in
      relocating to Kentucky. Mary reported that they dismantled their
      boats to build the first house in what is now Louisville, KY.
In Aug 1780, Jonathan joined Daniel Boone and others for a raid to
      "punish"the Shawnee Indians north of the Ohio River. He did
      not return from that venture, and probably died at the Battle of
      Piqua. Mary moved to her children to Harden County, KY and
      raised them there. Wm became a judge in Harden County.

1780 Colerain Twp

Maj. John Cessna, bn 1726   <John Cessna<the Frenchman   39/69
    Sarah Rose, bn ca 1740   39/
    Rachel Cessna, bn 1 Aug 1762   39/69
      (will marry Henry Williams 1 March 1781)
    John Cessna Jr, bn 8 Dec 1764   39/70
    Stephen Cessna, bn 28 Dec 1766   39/73
    Elizabeth Cessna, bn 1 Dec 1768   39/69
    William Cessna Esq, bn 20 June 1775   /69

1773 Colerain Twp Tax, John Cessna,   5.0
1774 Colerain Twp Tax, John Cessna,   6.5
1775 Colerain Twp Tax, John Cessna,   13.9
1776 Colerain Twp Tax, John Cessna,   12.1
July 1776, John is Major of Colerain Twp Militia
1779 Colerain Twp Tax, John Cesna, 400 acres, 5 horses, 6 cattle
1783 Colerain Twp, John Cessna Esq, 230 acres, 1 horse, 1 cow, 1 sheep

1784 Colerain Twp Tax, John Cisnaa Esq, 200 acres, no houses
      6 white souls
1783 Providence Twp Tax
      John Cessna, Esq,   600 acres, non-resident
      John Cissna, 100 acres, non-resident
1784 Providence Twp, John Cessna, 100 acres, no house, no one living
      on property
1785 Bedford County Tax John Cessna, Jr, 400 acres in Bedford Twp
      John Cessna, Esq, 200 acres in Colerain Twp
      John Cessna, single freeman, in CV twp.

Jonathan Cessna,   1780-1785   39/71
      bn 16 Nov 1760 <John<John<the Frenchman
Rebecca Worley-Cessna, bn 16 Aug 1764   39/71
      (Married 1779)
John Cessna Sr, bn 26 Aug 1780   /71
Stephen Cessna/Cisne, bn 17 April 1782   /71

1779 Colerain Twp Tax: Jonathan Cesna, 100 acres, 1 horse
1780-81 Colerain Twp Bedford County tax
      John Cessna Esq, Sheriff, 350 acres, 1 negro, 4 horses, 7 cows
      Jonathan Cessna, no land, 2 horses, 2 cows
1783 Colerain Twp, Jonathan Cessna, no acres, 2 horses, 4 cows, 1 sheep
1784 Colerain Twp, Jonathan Cisna, no acres, 4 white souls, no house
1784 Colerain Twp Bedford County, John Cessna, 200 acres, 20 corn
      saved? 3 horses & Mules, 4 horned cattle, 6 sheep
Note:1785 Jonathan moved to Cumberland Valley Twp., to the farm first
      warranted by Evans Cessna and Robert Hall.

1780 Cumberland Valley Twp

John Cessna, bn ca 1728   38/62
      <Charles<John<the Frenchman
Wife of John, bn ca 1760   38/62
John Cessna Jr, born ca 1780 (based on Georgia records)   38/62
Catherine Cessna, bn ca 1798 (killed by Indians in GA)   38/62

1773   Tax of Cumberland Valley twp, John Cessna   .6
1774   Tax Cumberland Valley twp, John Cessna   .5
1775   Tax Cumberland Valley twp, John Cessna   10.7
1776   Tax Cumberland Valley twp, John Cessna, uncultivated land,
      11shillings.3 pence, no provincial tax
1777, John Cessna Jr was pvt in Cumberland Valley Twp Militia Militia

1779 Tax Cumberland Valley twp, John Cessna Sr, 100 acres,
      no animals
1 Jan 1781, John Cessna, esq, took oath as sheriff of Bedford County.
      (In House of Cessna, Book I: Statement of Honorable John
      Cessna. He stated that his great grandfather, John Cessna was
      elected Sheriff of Bedford county in the years 1789-91-93).
21 Oct 1782, John Cessna, Esq appointed J.P. in Cumberland Valley
1783 Cumberland Valley twp, John Cessna Esq, 100 acres,
      no animals
      John Cisna Sr, 100 acres, non-resident (John of Shippensburg)
1784 Cumberland Valley Twp, John Cisna Esq, 100 acres, 1 house,
      3 whites

Note: This person has been assumed to be Major John Cessna. However,
Major John lives in the next township (Colerain) and has a
different population count in the 1784 census. Like Major John,
this person is given the honorific "Esquire" which indicates that
he had served a term as Judge, Sheriff, or lawyer. When
Colonel Charles Cessna relocated to Greene County, Georgia in
1786, this John disappeared from Bedford and became the first
Sheriff of that county. At the same time when John Cessna of
Colerain Township was listed as Major of the 1st Bedford
Battalion of Militia; this John was listed as a private in the
Cumberland Valley Militia under Colonel Charles Cessna. It is
obviously two different individuals.

Col. Charles Cessna, 1780-1784   38/57
      bn ca 1724   <John<the Frenchman
Elizabeth Culbertson-Cessna, bn ca 1743   38/57
Samuel Cessna, bn ca 1765   38/63
Elizbeth Cessna, bn ca 1774   38/63
Mary Cessna, bn ca 1764 (married Aaron Neel)   38/61
Robert Cessna, bn ca 1775   /61

1779 Cumberland Valley Twp Tax, Charles Cesna , 297 acres, 8 horses,
      3 cattle, 5 sheep
5 April 1780, Charles Cessna was appointed purchasing commissioner of
      Bedford County, posting 500£ bond
1783 Cumberland Valley twp Tax, Charles Cessna, 400 acres, 2 horses,
      4 cattle
1784 Cumberland Valley Twp Tax, Charles Cissna, 300 acres, 1 house,
      10 white souls, 1 black soul.

1784 Charles Cissna paid tax on 300 acres, 1 horse, 10 cattle, 1 sheep,
0 slaves; in CV twp.
Note: This is obviously Colonel Charles Cessna. He is second in
command of the 2nd Bedford Battn of Militia (Cumberland
Valley and West). In 1786, following charges which removed
him from a seat in the PA congress, Charles moved to Greene
County, GA. His 270 acre farm and property in Cumberland
Valley were sold to pay the bond he had posted for his duties as
County Commissioner.

Evan Cessna/Cissna, 1780-1784   39/69
     bn ca 1728-35   <John<the Frenchman
Mary Cissna, bn 1744   39/69
Thomas Cissna, bn 1764   39/69
Samuel Cissna, bn ca 1768   39/69
John Cissna, bn ca 1770   39/69
Robert Cissna, bn ca 1778   /69

1773   Cumberland Valley twp tax, Evan Cessna   .6
17 May 1773, Thomas Jones & Charles Cessna of Cumberland Cnty,
applied for 300 acres, including improvements, adjoining Robert
Hall & Evan Cessna on Branch of Evetts Creek, about 2 miles
from the block houses in Cumberland County.
1774   Tax Cumberland Valley twp, Evan Cessna, 0£.3sh.2 pence
1775   Tax   Cumberland Valley twp, Evan Cessna, .15.12
1776   Tax Cumberland Valley twp, Evan Cessna, .5.9
uncultivated land, . 6.0
1779   Tax Cumberland Valley twp, Evan Cessna, 200 acres, 3 horses,
5 cattle, 9 sheep
April 1779, Bedford County court session: Bernard Dougherty, Esq vs
William Wrong with notice to Evan Cissna, tenant in possession;
Ejectment.
1780-81 Tax Cumberland Valley Twp, Bedford County
Evin Cessna, 349 acres warranted, 2 horses, 4 cattle
1781, Evans was Capt in Cumberland Valley Militia
1782 Cumberland Valley Twp Tax, Bedford County
Capt. Evans Cessna, 140 acres Wtd, 1 horse, 1 mule, 2 horned cattle,
3 sheep
1783 Cumberland Valley Twp Tax, Capt. Evans Cesssna
150 acres warranted, 2 horses, 2 horned cattle
1.0.0 tax, 1 dwelling, 6 white children, 4 white women
1783 Cumberland Valley Twp, Even Cessna, 150 acres, 2 horse, 2 cattle
1784   Cumberland Valley Twp Tax, Even Cissna, 150 acres, 1 house,
7 white souls
Jan 1784, the tax collector made a note listing those who had "gone
away". It includes Charles Cessna and Evan Cessna.
1785,   Evan Cisney bought lot #223 in Pittsburgh for 13£.

1786, Westmoreland County, Pitt twp tax, Evan Cesna, .1.6
Note: 1784 Evan moved his family to Pittsburgh at the same time Col. Charles and family moved to Georgia.

Jonathan Cessna, bn 16 Nov 1760   **1785-1790**   39/67
                 <John<John<the Frenchman (Married 1779)
         Rebecca Worley-Cessna, bn 16 Aug 1764   /67
         John Cessna "Sr", bn 26 Aug 1780   /67
         Stephen Cessna/Cisne, bn 17 April 1782   /67

1785, Jonathan moved his family from Colerain Twp to the farm
         originally warranted to Robert Hall & Evan Cessna in
         Cumberland Valley twp. Purchased from Evan by
         Maj John Cessna in 1784.
1782 Cumberland Valley Twp tax Bedford County
         Jonathan Cessna, 100 acres warranted
1785 Bedford County tax Jonathan Cessna, 300 acres in CV twp

1780 Cumberland County

1780 Letterkenny Twp

William Cessna, bn ca 1742   44/73
              <John Cessna<the Frenchman
         Margaret Williamson, bn ca 174   44/73
         John Cessna, bn ca 1775   44/73
         Elizabeth Cessna, bn 30 Dec 1779   44/68
         Charles Cessna   /73

12-20-1770, William Cisney sold land in Middleton Twp to Robert
         Callender
July 1777, Wm. Cessna was 2nd Lt in militia from Franklin Twp
1779 Taxes for Letterkenny Twp Tax
         William Cessna, 170 acres, 2 horses, 2 cattle
1780 Letterkenny Supply Rates
         John Cisney, 170 acres, no other property
         William Cisney, 0 acres; 2 horses, 3 cattle, 0 negroes
1781 Letterkenny Twp Tax (father owns land but Wm is working it)
         William Cesney, no acres, 2 horses, 2 cattle
         John Cesney, 170 acres, no horses, no cattle.
1781, Wm Cessna was pvt 7th in Cpt James Culbertson's 3rd Co,
                 4 Battn Cumberland
1779 & 81 Letterkenny Twp Tax: William Cesna/Cesney

1779 Letterkenny Twp Cumberland County tax
       William Cessna,   170 acres $510 value
       2 horses $72/2 cows $24 value
1782 Letterkenny Twp Taxes
       John Cesney,   190 acres $213 value
       William Cesney,   1 horses $12 value
       2 cows $3/3 sheep $1   total value $16
9 Sep 1784, Lurgan and Letterkenny Twps. become Franklin County
Ca 1780, Charles Cessna married Rachel Culbertson

1780 Lurgan Twp

Theophilus Cisna, bn ca 1730 <Stephen<the Frenchman	43/75
Sarah Cissna, bn ca 1740	43/75
Thomas Cisna, bn ca 1760	43/75
William Cisna, bn ca 1764	43/74
Stephen Cisna, bn ca 1766	43/75
James Cisna, bn ca 1770	43/75
Stephen Cissna, bn 1755 <Thomas<Stephen<Frenchman	43/
(Theophilus' orphaned nephew)	

1780 Lurgan Supply Rates Cumberland County
       Theophelus Cesna   75 acres $100
              1 horse $15   1 cow $5
1 Mar 1781. Theophilus Cesna of Lurgan Twp was charged with keeping
      a Tippling House. (Drinking Establishment).
1781 Lurgan Twp Supply Rate Cumberland County
       Theop's Cisney   150 acres $125
       1 horse, $10; 2 cows $8   Total $143
1782 Lurgan Twp Taxes Cumberland County
       Theophelus Cesney, 150 acre $168
              2 horses $20 2 cows $8   Total $196
1785 Lurgan Taxes Franklin County
       Theophilis Cesna   1.15.3
1785-86 Lurgan and Letterkenny Twps are incorporated into Franklin Cty
1790 Census Franklin County, Lurgan Twp   Page 120 Theoflist Scisney
      2 males over 16, 2 males under 16, 2 females
22 Aug 1790 Theophilus Cesne is ensign in Cpt Wm. Strain's Co of 6th
      Battn Cumberland County, Lurgan Twp

1780 Peters Township

William W. Cissna Sr, bn ca 1760 Letterkenny twp.   44/63
        <William<John<The Frenchman
    Margaret ?   /63
    William W. Cessna Jr, bn 1780, Peters Township   /63
        <William<William<John<The Frenchman
    Sarah "Sally" Cessna, bn ca 1782   /63

Information taken from 1808, 1810, 1816, 1820, 1830, 1840, 1850
    Census of MS
1 Aug 1780, Wm Sisney was pvt 7th class in 3rd Company, 4th Battn of
    Cumberland County, Militia,Peters Twp, Franklin County.
1 Jul 1781, Wm. Cessna was pvt 7th class in Alexander Peebles Co. from
    Peters Twp, Franklin County. 3rd Company, 4th Battn,
    Cumberland County Militia
1784-1793, William was possibly of the Cessna migration to Greene
    County, GA.
1788, John Robinette and William Cessna served together in William
    Melton's Company of Horse Militia during the Indian uprising
    in Greene County, GA.

1780 Shippensburg

John Cessna, bn 1699 in Ireland <John<the Frenchman   42/72
    Theophilus Cessna, bn 1760   42/71
    James Cissna, Apr 1751   42/72
       Mary ?-Cessna, bn Feb 1749, wife of James   /72
       William Cessna, bn ca 1777   /72
       James Cessna, bn ca 1778   /72
       Mary Cessna, bn ca 1779   /72

Margaret Cessna, bn ca 1781 /72

    John Cessna, bn 1780 /72

    Sarah Cessna, bn 1782 /72

Mar 1780, James Cessna was Pvt in Militia from Hopewell Twp
Aug 1780, James Cessna was Pvt in militia from Hopewell Twp
1782 Hopewell Twp Taxes
        John Cessna, 1 house & lott, $269.10
        3 horses, $35, 2 cows, $8
1785   Shippensburgh Tax, John Cisney   0 acres, 4 horses, 4 cows,
        3 negroes, $150   Total: $599
1786 Shippensboro Tax
        John Cisna, 2 Lots, $70
        4 horses $40, 2 Cows $6, 2 negros $100 Total: $216
 1787 Shippensboro Twp Tax, Cumberland
        John Cisna,   1 house & 2 Lots $70
           3 negroes $130/3 horses & 2 cows $28.10 total $228.10
1788 Shippensboro Twp Tax, Cumberland County
        John Cisna, 2 Lots, $158
        2 Negroes $75, 4 horses & 2 cows, $46, total $279
1789 Shippensboro Twp Tax, Cumberland County
        John Cesna, 2 house & 3 lotts, $200
        1 Negro $30, 4 horses & 1 cow, $40, total $270
25 Sep 1780, Theophilus married Nancy Richardson in Chambersburg

Stephen Cissna, born 1755 43/68
    <Thomas<Stephen<the Frenchman
    Elizabeth Barnhill-Cissna, bn 1758 /68
    Mary "Polly Cissna, bn 1778 /68
    John Cissna, bn 1779 /68
    William Cissna, bn 1781

About 1789, Stephen moved the family to Pittsburgh. Elizabeth died the
    next year.
1778, Stephen Sisna was private in militia from Hopewell Twp
1781 Hopewell Twp tax
        John Cesna, no acres, 4 horses, 4 cattle, 1 negro
        Stephen Sisne, a taylor, no acres, no horses, 1 cattle
        (does this mean Stephen was renting farm, using animals
        that belonged to Uncle John?)

Charles Cessna, bn 1762   <William<John<the Frenchman 44/70
    Rebecca, bn ca 1764 (per daughter's gravestone) /70
        Married ca 1786

1779 Taxes for Hopewell Twp
    John Sisney, 150 acres, 4 horses, 3 cows, 2 negros
    Charles Sisney (listed on tax roll as living on farm,
    but with no property)
1779 Taxes for Hopewell Twp
    Charles Sisney, 1 town lot, $100
Note: Col. Charles Cessna (son of John) has been living in Cumberland
    Valley Twp for 15 years and cannot be this individual.

CENSUS 1790
The First Official US Census

1790 Georgia

1790 Greene County
originally Washington County
cluster of farms along Big Beaver Creek

Col. Charles Cessna, bn 1724 <John<the Frenchman   47 & 53/78
    Elizabeth Culbertson-Cessna, bn ca 1747   47 & 53/78
    Robert Cessna, bn ca 1775   47 & 53/78
    Mary Cessna, bn 1769   47 & 53/80

27 May 1790, Charles Cessna sold to Wm Wilson for 5£, an option to
    purchase 670 acres on waters of Richland creek.
1792, Charles Cessna was listed as JP in Greene County, GA (again in
    1793, 1794, 1795, 1796, 1798,)
1792, Mary Cessna married Aaron Neel in Greene County, GA
2 Sept 1795, Charles Cessna sold to Wm Wilson for 5£, option to
    purchase 670 acres on waters of Richland Creek of Oconee
    River. Witness by John Cessna, Sr, John Cessna, Jr and
    Samuel Cessna.

Unknown Cessna   bn ca 1768 <Charles<John<Frenchman   53/
    Wife,   53/
    Charles Cessna, bn 1785   /78
    Culbertson D. Cessna, bn 1787   /79
    Joseph Cessna, bn 1788   /79
    William S. Cessna, bn 1790   /79
    Elizabeth Cessna, bn ca 1786

Information taken from 1808, 1810, 1820, 1830 census.
Several family trees report that Elizabeth Cessna married John Robinette.
1811, Elizabeth Robinette witnessed document for Col Charles Cessna.
Mother of these children appears deceased in 1800 because by 1805
they are living with Col. Charles and Aaron Neel.

Note: All were born the years that the family was living in Greene County, GA. Because they are with Col Charles in Uttica, MS from 1808 until his death; they must be either children by a previously unidentified son, **OR** they indicate that Col. Charles remarried to a much younger woman soon after moving to Georgia. For this book, I have assumed they are his grandchildren.

John Cessna, bn ca 1750   <Charles<John<the Frenchman   48 & 52/83
   Mary Cessna, bn ca 1750 wife of John Cessna   48/83
   John Cessna Jr, bn 1770   48/83
   Catherine Cessna, bn ca 1775   48/

1786, John Cessna received land grant in Washington County, GA (land was granted first to veterans of Rev War)

1786, John Cessna warranted 500 acres, Washington County

1788, John Cessna warranted 1000 acres, Washington County

31 Dec 1789, John Rice of Green County sold to Moses Shelby for 60£, 453 acres on Big Beaverdam of Richland Creek, adjoining John Cessna.

11 Jan 1790. Bond posted for John Cessna, Sheriff elect of Greene

10 Mar 1789, Lost letters at PO: M. Meals to Merriwether in file of Jn. Cessina

1789 Georgia Tax Digest: Greene County/Melton twp, John Cesna County, for $5,000. Surities were posted by William Melton, Moses Shelby & Thomas Baldwin. Oath taken before H. Osborn. (listed as sheriff in 1791, 1792, 1793, 1794, 1798)

18 Jan 1790, John Cessna of Greene County sold to David Culbertson of Wilkes County for £80, 400 acres on Beaverdam, part of 500 acres granted to John Cessna, 24 May 1786, bounded by John Dunn and Lester's line. Witness by Moses Shelby, John McMichael & William Patrick

13 July 1792, John Cessna filed Notice that the Jail he was responsible for cannot safely keep prisoners from escaping and he has no ability to repair it.

Sep 1793, Catherine Cissna, a young lady, was cruelly murdered by Indians just outside Greenville, GA.

2 Sept 1795, Charles Cessna sold to Wm Wilson for £5, option to purchase 670 acres on waters of Richland Creek of Oconee River. Witness by John Cessna, Sr, John Cessna, Jr and Samuel Cessna.

1797, John moved to Buncombe County, NC; along French Broad River where it meets the Tennessee state line.

Samuel Cessna, bn ca 1760   48 & 53/
   <Col. Charles<John<the Frenchman
 Polly Baker-Cessna, bn ca 1766   48/77
 Samuel Cessna Jr, bn ca 1790   48/77
 Elizabeth Cessna, bn ca 1787   48/77
 Robert Cessna, bn ca 1784   48/77

1786, Polly Cessna was attacked and scalped. "The first casualty of the Indian wars in Greene County was Mrs. Cessna who was scalped alive by the Indians while her husband was clearing land for planting. She crossed the Oconee river at "Cow Ford" and warned the settlers. These gave pursuit of the savages and killed them."
1784 Head rights granted to early county residents: Samuel Sessney, 220 Acres on Richland Creek
3 April 1788, petition to Governor from inhabitants of Greene County, GA asking for a Company of Horse under Captain William Melton to defend the frontier. Samuel Cisney signed.
1789 Georgia Tax Digest: Greene County/Melton twp, Samuel Cessna
3 Dec 1792, Samuel Cessna witness for Power of Attny given for Edward Peters.
22 Mar 1793, Samuel Cessna of Greene County, traded a negro woman named Agg and her daughter, Hannah, for a negro boy, Isaac. Female negroes were estate of Robert Baker, left to Polly Baker, traded to Thomas Baldwin. Wit James Taylor

James Milligan
 Elizabeth Cessna-Milligan, bn ca 1774   47 &54/80
   <Col Charles<John<the Frenchman
 John Cessna Milligan, bn 2 Dec 1789   /80

8-19-1788 Elizabeth Cessna married James Milligan in Greene County GA

William W. Cissna Sr, bn ca 1760 Letterkenny twp. 57/74
   <William<John<The Frenchman
 Margaret ?   57/74
 William W.Cessna Jr, bn 1780, Peters Township 57/74
 Sarah "Sally" Cessna. bn ca 1780   57/74

28 Aug 1794, William Cessna of Greene County sold to Jno Michel, for 20£, 62 acres on water of Oconee River. Margaret Cessna signed to relinquish widow's rights. Cessna bought the land from Wm. Wilson.

6 Nov 1795, William Cessna of Greene County sold to James Morgan of
 same county for £20, 280 acrs on waters of Oconee River, part
 of a tract where William Cessna now lives, and part of a 670
 Acres granted to Charles Cessna on 19 Aug 1788.
13 Aug 1796 William Wilson made a Quit Claim Deed, testifying that
 he had sold a certain tract of land on waters of Oconee to
 William Cessna who has since sold the land to James Morgan.
 In exchange for the Quit Claim, Cessna is to deliver a young
 cow and Calf.
1799, William Cessa and John Robinett moved their families to
 Muhlenberg County, KY....then to Mississippi about 1802.
Information taken from 1808, 1810, 1816, 1820, 1830, 1840, 1850 Census of MS

1790 KENTUCKY

1790 Hardin County

Mary Friend-Cessna, bn ca 1755 Widow of Jonathan Cessna   51/77
 William Cessna, bn 17 June 1776   51/77
   <Jonathan<John<Frenchman
 Nancy Agnes Cessna, bn ca 1774   51/77
   <Jonathan<John<Frenchman

15 July 1783, Mary Cisnea had 200 acres surveyed on Hinches Run in
 Jefferson County, KY. (William Hinch was Mary's Bro-in-law).
6 Aug 1782, Inventory of Jonathan Cessna: 1 Dark Bay Mare £20 a Red
 Cow £4.10; a spotted cow 4£, a spotted haffer 3£; 1 ewe £.12;
 three pewter dishes, 8 pewter plates, 4 pewter basins, spoons and
 cups, a frying pan, 2 pots, 1 spinning wheel; a broad axe and 4
 old axes, 1 rifle gun; Utensils for husbandry, pot hooks &
 lumber; a hackle, a side saddle, books, a bead and beading, a
 bead and comforter.
24 Oct 1785, Jonathan Friend, Brother of Mary Friend-Cessna was
 given authority to sell their farm outside Bedford PA.
1790 Nancy Agnes Cessna was given permission to marry Shepherd Gum
 in Hardin County, KY by her mother, Elizabeth.

1790 MICHIGAN

1796 River Rouge area
Not included in 1790 census because Detroit area
was under British control until 1796

William Cissna, born 1773 <Joseph <John Cessna<the Frenchman   50/82
No family listed in 1796 Census
Late in the 1790's William purchased Lot 35 of River Rouge
French Ribbon farms, 271.84 acres

James Cissna, born 1776   <Joseph <John Cessna<the Frenchman   50/78
No family listed in 1796 Census
Late in the 1790's James purchased Lot 43 of River Rouge French
Ribbon farms, 277.6 acres

John Cissna, born 1774 <Joseph <John Cessna<the Frenchman   50/82
No family listed in 1796 Census
Late in the 1790's John purchased Lots 32 & 49 of River Rouge French
Ribbon farms, 271.33 acres; and Lot 660, 301.6

Joseph Cissna, born ca 1747 <John Cessna<the Frenchman   50/81
  Rebecca Cissna, born ca 1750   2nd wife of Joseph   /81
    Married about 1786
  Sarah Cissna, bn 1782 (will marry Godfrey Corbus)   50/81
  Stephen P. Cissna, bn 1787   /81
  Joseph Cissna, bn 24 June 1789   /81
  David Cissna, bn 1790   /81
  Evans Cissna, bn ca 1792   /81

1796, When the British surrendered Detroit to the Americans
    Joseph Cissna became one of the first Justices of the Peace for
    Wayne County in Michigan Territory.
14 & 15 Jan 1790, Roll of the Election held at Detroit: Joseph
    Cisney & William Cisney voting for Jacob Visger &
    Oliver Wiswell
15 July 1796, First US Census made of Michigan Trr: **Joseph Cisanney**
    Male over 16,   Joseph Cessna bn 1747
    Male under 16, *Evans Cissna*?
    Male under 16, *Stephen P. Cissna*
    Male under 16, *Joseph Cissna* bn 1789
    Female,   Rebecca Cissna
    Female,   Sarah Cissna (Corbus)
    Female ?

William Cissaney, /81
  separate household (no count, just his name)
James Cisanney, /82
  separate household (no count, just his name)

15 July 1796, Census taken of the Company of River Rouge Taken by
  Gabl. Godfroy, Lt. Jn. And ensign John Cisanney, Joseph
  Cisanney, 1 male over 16, 3 males under 16, 3 females
  In household: William, and James Cisanney, Samuel Driverd

1790 NORTH CAROLINA

1790 Guilford County
Horse Pen Creek Farms

Stephen Sisney, bn 1745   <John<Stephen<the Frenchman
  Stephen Sisney, bn 1745 in York County, PA 49/84
  Dolly Holton-Sisney, bn ca 1756 49/84
  Robert Cisney, bn ca 1788 49/84
  Elizabeth Sisney (-Rea), bn 1785 49/84
  Mary Sisney, bn ca 1785 49/84
  William Stephen Sisney, will be born 1794 /84
  John "Scotty" Sisney, will be born 2 June 1796 /84

May 1787, Aron Mondingall proved a deed from Daniel Brittan
    and wife, to Stephen Sisna, in Guilford County, 60 acres in
    Guilford County, NC; on the waters of Horsepen Creek;
    "includes improvement he is now in possession of".
 1789, Stephen Sisney entered 60 acres in Guilford County, on waters of
    Horse Pen Creek.
27 Nov 1793, North Carolina granted 50 acres in Guilford County along
    Brush Creek at cost of 10£ per 100 acres, to Stephen Cisney.
18 Nov 1797, Stephen Cisney sold 110 acres at same location to Jesse
    Dillon for 40£. Land is near Coffins Corners on waters of Horse
    Pen and Brush Creeks. Two tracts make up the 110 acres.
 1797, Revolutionary War veterans of North Carolina were able to
    apply for bounty land grants in the newly formed Christian
    County in South Central Kentucky. Following his service
    1781-82, Stephen was a veteran of the Continental Army.

1798, Stephen Sisney moved his family along Pond River in what would eventually become Christian, then Todd County, KY.

John Taylor, bn ca 1765
 John Taylor, bn ca1765
 Rachael Sisney-Taylor, bn ca 1773   49/84
  <Stephen and Dolly<John<Stephen<the Frenchman
 Male under 16 **Son**, born 1785-90
 Female under 16 **Daughter** born 1785-90

Rachael married John Taylor about 1785.

Joseph/John Sisney, bn ca 1749   49/
 wife of Joseph, bn ca 1755-60
 Son, bn 1780-90
 Son, bn 1780-90
 Daughter, bn 1780-90
 Daughter, bn 1780-90

Note: Census states the name is "Joseph" but dates and information from Quaker Records indicate this is John, son of John and Pryscilla. The location of this family after 1790 has not been found.

1790 Pennsylvania

1790 Allegheny County
1790 Pitt Twp

Stephen Signney   \<Thomas\<Stephen\<the Frenchman

Stephen Cissna, bn 20 July 1755	58/85
Elizabeth Barnhill-Cissna, bn 1758 married 1793	58/
John Cissna, bn 1779	58/85
Charles Cissna, bn 1783	/85
William Cissna, bn 1781	58/85
James Cissna, bn 1789	/85
Mary "Polly"Cissna, bn 1787	/85

Male over 16:
White Female:
White Female:
White Female:

NOTE: Stephen was an Innkeeper in both Pittsburgh and Chillicothe.
So the extra people may or may not be relatives. Stephen Cissna
is the orphaned son of Thomas and Margaret Cisney; born in
Carlisle. Stephen fought with Robert Cluggage in the early days
of the Revolutionary War. Stephen remarried about 1791 to
Margaret Millicent Hegan, listed as a "Spinster". About 1799,
he moved his family to Chillicothe, Ohio Territory.

1791 Allegheney County Tax, Pitt Twp, Steven Cesna,   1.8

1789 through 1792, Stephen Cissna was very active in politics and served
on a number of Grand Juries,

1792, Stephen was listed among the many people keeping Taverns in
Pittsburgh.

3 Sep 1793, Stephen Cessna married Margaret Hegan, and on they
sold ½ of lot #202 for 50£. At some point Stephen and Margaret
also purchased lot #223 from Evans and Mary.

23 February 1796, James Morrison (an attorney from KY), using power
of attny for Stephen Cisnay, sold lot #223 and all houses and
buildings to Ebenezer Finnamore for 165 £. Stephen has already
moved to Chillicothe, OH; but Margaret is still living in
Pittsburgh.

1787, Signers of a petition to form Allegheny County.
        Stephen Cisna on page 3…James Cissna on page 7

1787 Tax for Pitt Township, Westmoreland County, PA
        Evan Cesna, 0.0.9

Stephen Cesna,   0.0.7
1790 Census of Allegheny County Pitt Twp
   Stephen Signney: 2 White males over 16, 4 white males under
14, 5 free white females
John Chesney: 1 white male over 1, 2 free white females

Capt. Evans Cissna, bn ca 1728 \<John\<the Frenchman	54/87
Mary Cissna, bn ca 1755	54/87
Samuel Cissna, bn ca 1781	54/87
Thomas Cissna, bn ca 1778	54/85
John Cissna, bn ca 1780	54/88
Robert Cissna, bn ca 1788	54/85

8 May 1787, Evan Cisney bought Lot #209, town of Pittsboro,
   from Wm Braden and wife Rosanna for 5 shillings. Baden
   bought the lot from John Penn and John Penn Jr. Lot on 2nd and
   Front Streets.
He **was not listed** in the 1790 Census but he owned property.
1Sep 1785, Evans and Mary Cisney purchased lot #223 for 13£. 8 May
1787, Evans and Mary Cisney purchased lots #209 and #210 on
   Second Street, for 5 shillings (about $1) each.
10 Oct 1791, they sold lot #210 to Margaret Millicent Hegan (described
   in the deed as a spinster). Margaret already owned lot #202.

1790 Bedford County

This was a page by page, line by line search
of the micro filmed version of the Census.
Not all townships were available.

1790 Colerain Twp.
Rainsburg, PA

John Cislor   \<John\<Jean de Cesna

Major John Cessna, bn 26 Jan 1726	51/90
Elizabeth Hall Cessna, bn 1 Dec 1768	/90
Elizabeth Cessna, bn 1 Dec 1768	51/90
William Cessna, bn 20 June 1775	/90
Charles Cessna, bn 10 Mar 1789	/90
Evans Cessna, 2 Oct 1792	/90

Sarah Rose, bn 1791 /90
Henry Cessna, bn ca 1795 /90
James Cessna, bn 1797 /90
Robert Hall, bro-in-law
White female: (*possibly Mrs. Hall*) to help take care of the
infant Charles

15 Oct 1795, Will of Samuel Hall of Colerain twp, a mason, "at present in
a very low state" in the home of Son-in-law, John Cessna. John
to keep his son Robert until he reaches 21.
21 June 1794, John Cessna, Sr, bought 400 a, Bedford co,
17 Aug 1786, Colerain Twp Bedford County Tax
John Cissna, 205 acres, 2 horses, 4 horned cattle
Single Freemen in Colerain twp: John Cissna
1787 Colerain Twp Tax, Bedford County
John Cesna Jr, 350 acres warranted, no livestock, value 300
John Cessna Jr, 100 acres warranted, 2 horses, 3 cattle, value 250
John Cessna Esq, 205 acres warranted, 2 horses, 4 cattle, value 350
John Cessna Sen, 100 acres, 2 horses, 4 horned cattle, value 330
1788 Colerain Twp Tax, Bedford County
John Cessna Sr, 205 acres warranted, 3 horses, 3 cattle, value 202
John Cissna Jr., no acres, 1 horse, 1 cattle
John Cessna Esq, under nonresidents
1791 Colerain Twp Tax, Bedford County
John Cessna Jr, 200 acres warranted, 3 horse, 4 cattle
1796 Colerain Twp Tax, Bedford County
John Cisna, 400 acres warranted, 3 horses, 2 cattle
1797 Colerain Twp Tax, Bedford County, John Cessna, $6
1798 Coleraine Twp Tax, Bedford County, John Cesna, $4
1790 Census Bedford County, Colerain twp.
John Scisney, 2 males over 16, 3 females.Next to Edward Rose
1795, Elizabeth Cessna married William Vickory

John Scisney <John<John<the Frenchman
John Cessna, bn 8 Dec 1764 51/89
Mary McCaulsin-Cissna, 2 Mar 1768 /89
Sally Cessna, bn 6 May 1788 /89
Margaret Cessna, bn 6 Sep 1789 /89
Male over 16: ??? could be a brother or hired man. /89

Their infant son, John Cessna, was born in Feb 1787 and died in April.
1789 Colerain Twp tax, Bedford County
John Cissna Jr, no acres, 2 horses, 1 cattle
22 Apr 1792, John Cessna Jr was appointed guardian of Eleanor & John
Tantlinger, children of Henry Tantlinger dec'd.

1790 Cumberland Valley Township

Jonathan Scisney   <John<John<the Frenchman

Jonathan Cessna, bn 16 Nov 1760	52/91
Rebecca Worley-Cessna, bn 16 Aug 1769	52/91
(wife of Jonathan)	
John Cessna, bn 26 Aug 1780	52/91
Stephen Cessna, bn 17 Apr 1782	52/91
Charles Cessna, bn 8 Feb 1784	/91
Jonathan Cessna Jr, bn 1 Apr 1789	/91
Sarah Cessna, bn 11 Nov 1786	/87

White female: *this could be Rebecca's mother.

> 16 June 1794, Jonathan Cessna, 400 a, Bedford County
> 1795, Thomas & Sarah Worley, children of Echor Worley dec'd,
> both above the age of 14, ask the court for Jonathan
> Cessna to be their guardian.

Stephen Cessna, <John<John<the Frenchman   51/93

> 5 Dec 1789, John Cessna of Colerain Twp, for 230£ sold to Stephen
> Cessna of Colerain Twp, a tract of land lying in Cumberland
> Valley known by the name of Mount Pleasant on Dogwood
> Ridge and Spice Bottoms; bounded on the south by lands of
> John Elder; on the North by lands of John Cessna the elder; and
> on the East and West by vacant land: containing 173 ½ acres.
> The same now being in possession of Adam Butcher. There is
> no indication that Stephen actually lived on this farm. The next
> item suggest he used it as a rental property.
> 1789 Colerain Twp Tax, Bedford County
> Stephen Cissna, 205 acres warranted, 2 horses, 2 cattle
> Single Freemen: Steven Cesna
> 1790 Census lists Stephen as a "Single Freeman" living in Colerain Twp.
> But deeds show that he owns land in Cumberland Valley Twp.
> 9 Sep 1797, Stephen Cessna of Toboyne Twp., for 600£, sold to
> John Alguire of Cumberland Valley Twp in Bedford County, a
> tract of land now in possession of John Alguire; situated in the
> Township of Cumberland Valley, by survey to be 175 acres of
> land; joining lands of John Elder, Ezekiel Cox and Samuel
> Walkman; subject to payment of arears and Interest due.

Henry Williams

Rachel Cessna-Williams, 1 Aug 1762		51/90
<John<John<Frenchman		
Hannah Williams, bn 24 May 1782		
John Williams, bn 30 Aug 1784		/90
Sarah "Sally" Williams, bn 1 Jul 1786		/90
Margaret P. Williams, bn 25 Feb 1789		/90
Elizabeth Williams, bn 12 Apr 1791		/90
Rebecca Williams, bn 4 Mar 1794		/90
Rachael Williams, bn 9 Apr 1797		/90
Mary Williams, bn 11 Mar 1800		/90
Eleanor "Nellie" Williams, bn 6 Oct 1802		/90

20 Mar 1781, Rebecca Cessna married Henry Williams
House of Cessna family reports.

1790 Cumberland County

1790 Hopewell Township

James Scisney <John<the Frenchman	58/92
James Cessna, bn April 1751	58/92
Mary ?-Cessna, bn ca 1781 wife of James	58/92
William Cessna, bn ca 1777	58/92
James Cessna, bn ca 1779	58/92
John Cessna, bn 1780	58/92
Mary Cessna, daughter of James	58/92
Margaret Cessna, daughter of James	58/92
Sarah Cessna, daughter of James	58/92
John Cessna, father of James	58/
bn ca 1699 in Ireland, d 1796	
Elizabeth Cessna, bn 30 Dec 1779,	49/86
daughter of James' brother William	
Slaves: 2	

1793, description of properties and value in Shippensburg:
James Cissna lot on King Street value $50
James Cissna, Southampton Twp, House & lot,
22x24 made of wood $850 Samuel Tate (tenant)
& kitchen 16x16, made of wood, $2112
William McKnight, Stable 18x20, made of wood

James Cissna, house & lot occupied by Widow Miller, 12x20, made of wood, $120
1793 Census of Shippensburg listed James Sisna as a farmer.
30 Sep 1796, John Cessna, son of the Frenchman, died.

1790 Toboyne Township
becomes part of Perry County, PA

John Gardner Sr 2-1-4
    John Gardner Sr
    John Gardner Jr
    Stephen Cisna, bn 28 Dec 1766   51/89
                 <John<John<the Frenchman
    Nancy Gardner-Cisna, bn ca 1768   /89
    Mrs John Gardner Sr
    White female
    White female

12 April 1790, Stephen Cisney of Bedford County married Mary
        Gardner of Centre in Cumberland County. At the Centre
        Presbyterian Church. This community will become a part of
        Perry County. Later, her father, John Gardner sold them a
        farm near his in Toboyne twp. They named it Cisna Run.
1793 Census of Toboyne twp, Cumberland County PA
27 Jan 1789, Stephen Cessna was a resident of Colerain Twp.

1790 Franklin County
1790 Letterkenny Twp

William Cessna, bn ca 1741 <John<Frenchman   55/86
    Margaret Williamson, wife of William   55/
    John Cessna, bn ca 1771 <William<John<Frenchman   55/85
    Charles Cessna, <William<John<the Frenchman   55/91
    Rachel Cessna, wife of Charles   /86
    Rebecca Cessna, ca 1790   d/0 Charles   /87

2 Aug 1790, US Census does not list either William or Charles Cessna as still living at the farm on Culbertson's Row. It does however list all five of the neighbors identified in the Oct 11th deed to Winger. It is not known where these two families were living at the time.

6 Feb 1787, William Cissna, bought 230 acres in Franklin County,

21 Jun 1794, Charles Cissna made a claim of 400 acres in Bedford County. Family history reports he moved to Bedford County at that time. Note: 30 Jul 1837 Charles Cessna died in Bedford County. His family later add his name to a plaque at the Old Presbyterian Cemetery identifying him as Col. Charles Cessna. His daughter's grave marker states that his wife's name was Rachel (not Elizabeth Culbertson as recorded in House of Cessna).

11 October 1790, John Cessna sold a farm he had held for over 40 years to his son William Cessna. It was described as being in Letterkenny Twp of Franklin County: bounded by Bounded by lands of Sam Culbertson, John Naves, Michael Naves, George Groves, William Kilpatrick & Jacob Naves. In his Will, John Cessna mentioned that he got this land from Nathanial Wilson.

17 Dec 1790, William Cessna and wife Margaret, sold this farm to Abraham Winger for 650£.

1790 Lurgan Township

William Cisney, bn 1764 <Theophilus<Stephen<the Frenchman   56/95
   Wife of William Cisna, bn 1768   /95
   James Cisna, bn ca 1788   /95
   George Cisna,

William pvt in company of Capt William Strain's, 22 days in 1781, this unit was from Lurgan Twp in Franklin County.

Sons: James & George (From House of Cessna)

1 Nov 1786, William Cisna requested 230 acres, including an improvements and adjoining land of Samuel Culbertson, William Kirkpatrick and John Knave in Letterkenny Township.

1790 Hopewell Twp
(to become Southhampton Twp)
near Orrstown

Theophilist Scisney   <Stephen<the Frenchman
    Theophilis Sisney/Cisna, bn ca 1730   56/88
    Sarah Cessna, wife of Theophilus   56/88
    James Cisna, bn ca 1781   56/88
    Stephen Cisna, bn ca 1767-70   56/95
    Margaret, *Wife of Stephen*   /95
    Theophilus Cisna, bn ca 1789   /95
        son of Stephen & Margaret Cisna

10 May 1778, Theopholus Cisna, was ensign in company of Capt
    William Strain 6th Battalion Cumberland Co.
1778-1783 Theops. Cesna, Captain in Northampton County Rangers, lists
    he was from Cumberland Cty.

1790 Lurgan Twp
Farm near Fannetsburg, PA

Theophilus Cessna, bn 1760 <John<The Frenchman   52/95
    Sarah Cessna, bn 1776 d 1790   /95
        Married 25-Sep-1780
    Betsy Cessna, bn ca 1790-1800   /95
    James Cessna, bn ca 1790-1800   /95

Jan 1785, Theophilus Cisna applied for 300 acres of land in Southampton
    Twnship of Franklin County, adjoining lands of Robert
    Shameson, Casper Lee, Jacob Hoover, John Barns and others.
1786 Taxes Southampton twp, Franklin Co: Theophilus Cessna.
    Samuel Culbertson. John Culbertson. Southamption Twp,
    Franklin County....was originally part of Lurgan until 1783
6 Feb 1787, Theophilus Cisna claims 300 acres in Franklin County
John Cessna Sr, sold to Theophilius Cessna, 100 acres for 100 pounds,
    near Shippensburg. Deeded in 1790. John got the land before
    1756. 20 April 1796 Theophiles and wife Sarah, of Fannet Twp
    sell this land in Southampton Twp to John Breckenridge

1789, Theophilus Cisna paid tax in Southampton Twp of Franklin
County 0.19.10
31 Oct 1792, Return of officers of Franklin County Militia, 4th
Company of 5th Regiment, Capt. Theophilus Cissna

1790 Fannett Twp

Thomas Cisna,   <Theophilist<Stephen<the Frenchman

Thomas Cisna, bn ca 1761		50/94
Wife of Thomas Cisna, bn ca 1767		/94
Theophilus J. Cissna, bn ca 1782		/96
Thomas Henderson Cissna, bn ca 1787		/94
Archibald Cisna, bn ca 1789		/94
John Alfred Cisna, bn ca 1785		/94
William Henry Cisna, bn ca 1787		/94
David Alexander Cisna, bn ca 1789		/94

1778-1783, Thomas Cessna, was ensign in company of Thos Asky of
Cumberland County of Rangers,
15 April to 15 June 1781 Thomas Cissna was ensign on Capt. Tomas
Askey's Payroll, Cumberland Co. Militia. Fannet twp, Franklin
County. Note: Payroll indicates that he was on active duty.
Militia Roll is a list of men living in the Twp; but does not
indicate if they actually served active duty.
1798 Tax for Franklin County, Thomas Cisna renting from Wm
McIntire, Thomas Cisna, 1 house, 2 acres. Fannet Twp
10 May 1816, Heirs of Thomas Cisna file for Bounty Land Warrant.
Sons: Thomas Henderson Cisna. Archibald Cisna, Theophilus J.
Cisna, John Alfred Cisna, William Henry Cisna, David
Alexander Cisna. (From House of Cessna)

1790 Peters Twp

William W. Cessna, bn ca 1760	51/79
Wife	51/79
William W. Cessna Jr, bn ca 1780	51/79
Sarah "Sally" Cessna, bn ca 1782	51/79

Based on ages in 1810 & 1820 census of MS
1802, Sally Cessna married James Sharp in Muhlenberg County, KY

1800 CENSUS
1800 Census was destroyed in War of 1812

1800 Georgia
1800 Greene County

Polly Baker-Cessna, bn ca1765   63/97
     Widow of Samuel<Charles<John<the Frenchman
Samuel Cessna Jr, bn ca1784   63/97
Robert Baker Cessna, bn ca1786   63/97
Elizabeth Cessna, bn ca1788   63/97

     1784, Head rights granted to early county residents:
         Samuel Sessney, 220 Acres on Richland Creek
     1784, Head rights granted to early county residents
         Charles Cessna, 670 Acres on Richland Creek
     3 June 1797, Mary Cessna and John file for administration on
         estate of Samuel Cessna.
     1803, Polly re-married to John Royston

1800 Kentucky
1800 Hardin County

Mary Friend-Cessna, bn ca 1755, Widow of Jonathan Cessna   64/98
William Cessna, bn 17 June 1776   <Jonathan<John<the Frenchman   64/98

Sheperd Gum
     Nancy Agnes Cessna-Gum,   64/99
         bn ca 1774 <Jonathan<John<the Frenchman

1800 Muhlenberg County

Robert Cessna, bn 1775 <Charles<John<the Frenchman   61/99
    Elizabeth Culbertson-Cessna, bn ca 1780   /99
    Elizabeth Hester "Eliza" Cessna, bn ca1795   /99
    Mary E. Cessna, bn ca 1798   /99

28 May 1799, Robert Cissna was appointed J.P. of Muh County
25 June 1799, Robert Cisna registered his stock mark
26 Aug 1800, Robert Cissna, esq had vacated JP position.
23 Mar 1801, Robert Cessna claimed right to 200 acres on Green River
12 Oct 1796, Robert Cisna had 200 acres surveyed.
12 Oct 1803, Robert Cisna had 200 acres survened on Nelson creek
22 Apr 1805, Robert Cesna paid tax on 400 acres on Green River
28 June 1799, Taxes for Muhlenberg County: Robert Cessna,
        200 acres on Nelson's creek: 1/0/0/0/2/0
   John Culbertson, 200 acres on Nelson's Creek: 1/1/0/2/5/0
   Joseph Culbertson, no land 1/0/0/0/1/0
1800 Taxes of Muhlenberg County KY
   July 11 John Culbertson, 200 acres on Green river, patented to John
      Culbertson 2 white males over 21, 1 white over 16, 1 black over
      16, 3 blacks under 18, 8 total
   July 11 Robert Cessna, 200 acres on Green River,   Patented to
      Robert Cessna 1 white male over 21, ……..5 total.
1801 Census of Muhlenberg County
   Apr 14, John Culbertson, 200 acres on Green river, One WM over
      21; 2 WM over 16; 1 Black over 16; 3 Blacks total; 8 horses
   Apr 14, Joseph Culbertson, no land: Four WM over 21; no WM over
      16; no Blacks over 16; no Blacks; 2 horses
   Apr 14 Robert Cessna. 200 acres on Green river One WM over 21; No
      WM under 16;1 Black over 16; 2 Blacks; 4 horses

Col Charles Cessna, bn 1724   <John<the Frenchman   61/101
    Elizabeth Culbertson-Cessna, bn ca 1724   61/
    Charles Cessna, bn 1783   61/102
        <unknown<Charles<John<Frenchman
    Culbertson D. Cessna, bn 1785   61/102
        <unknown<Charles<John<Frenchman
    Joseph Cessna, bn 1787   61/102
        <unknow<Charles<John<Frenchman
    William S. Cessna,   **bn 1790**   61/102
        <unknown<Charles<John<Frenchman

3 March 1801, Census of Muhlenberg County
Charles Cessna, 200 acres, One WM over 21; 2 blacks above
16; 4 blacks total; 2 horses
Information taken from 1808, 1810, 1820, 1830 census.
Parents of these boys appear deceased in 1800 because by 1805 they are
living with Col. Charles and Aaron Neel.
23 Mar 1801, Charles Cissna claimed right to land on Cypress Ck, 200 ac
18 Oct 1805, Charles Cissna sold his 200 acres on Cypress to Peter
Watkins
There is no evidence that Elizabeth Culbertson-Cessna was still living.

William W. Cissna Sr, bn ca 1760 Letterkenny twp.   76/103
   <William<John<The Frenchman
Margaret   76/103
William W. Cessna Jr, bn 1780,   76/104
   <William<William<John<The Frenchman
Sarah "Sally" Cessna, bn ca 1780   59/100

Information taken from 1808, 1810, 1816, 1820, 1830, 1840, 1850 Census of MS
25 June 1799, William Cisna registered his stock mark
25 June 1799, William Cissna & Henry Davis ordered to mark Road from
John Culbertson's ford on Green River to Greenville.
23 July 1799, William Cisna was member of first grand jury in
Muhlenberg County.
28 Jan 1800, Wm Cissna, John Robinet & John Bradley ordered to mark
a road from Bradley's Horse Mill to intersect road from
Lewisburg to Greenville.
1800, Muhlenburg County Tax, Robert Cestna and William Cestna
Apr 1802, James Sharp married Sally Cesna
1800 Taxes of Muhlenberg County KY
   July 10 William Cessna 200 acres, Cyprus Creek, patented to William
   Cessna, 1 white male above 21; no whites; 1 black above 16;
   total blacks 1; no horses or cows
   July 10 William Cessna 200 acres, Cyprus Creek , Patented to John
   Robinette
   1801 Census of Muhlenberg County
   March 8, William Cessna, 200 acres, One WM over 21; 2 WM over
   16; 6 horses

James Milligan
Elizabeth Cessna-Milligan, bn ca 1766   63/99
   <Charles<John<the Frenchman
John C Milligan, bn 20 Dec 1789   63/99
Metilda Milligan, bn 22 Mar 1792   /99
Melinda Milligan, bn 1 Jul 1795   /99
Charles Milligan, bn 20 Jan 1800   /99

19 Aug 1788, Elizabeth Cessna married James Milligan in Greene Cty, GA. Matilda Milligan, bn 25 Sep 1795, appears to have died in infancy.

1799, Family moved to Muhlenberg County, KY with Elizabeth's father.

Aaron Neel   /103
>**Mary Cessna-Neel,** bn ca 1769   61/103
>><Charles<John<the Frenchman
>
>**Aaron Lovett Neel,** bn ca 1793   /103
>**Charles Cessna Neel,** bn ca 1795   /103
>**Robert Cessna Neel,** bn ca 1797   /103
>**Thomas S. Neel,** bn ca 1799   /103
>**Elizabeth Neel,** bn ca 1801   /103
>**Caroline Neel,** bn ca 1803   /103
>>*(married Gibeon Gibson Tidwell)*   /103
>
>**Lurenna Smith Neel,** born ca 1804   /103

Aaron Neel moved to Muhlenberg County, KY about 1799, then to Jefferson County, Mississippi by 1802. All of these children moved to Madison County, Mississippi in the early 1830's. Aaron Lovett Neel and Charles C. Neel stayed in Madison County and are buried there in marked graves. Thomas S. Neel moved back to Hinds County, MS and was buried there. Robert C. Neel moved to Arkansas.

1800 Taxes of Muhlenberg County KY
>July 11, Aaron L. Neel, on Nelson Creek

1800 Michigan

1800 Detroit Area
River Rouge

Joseph Cissna, bn 1747 <John<the Frenchman   65/
  Rebecca Cissna, bn ca 1750   65/
    Stephen P. Cissna, bn 1785   65/101
    Joseph Cissna, bn 24 June 1789   /101
    David Cissna   /101
    Evans Cissna   65/100

15 July 1796, First US Census taken after British surrender Detroit and Michigan Territory. Joseph Cisanney, James Cisanney, William Cissanney.

15 Jan 1799, Election roll of Detroit listed William Cisney and Joseph Cisney

20 Jan 1800, Governor St. Clair removed Joseph Cissna and James May as Justices of the Peace over a disagreement in election results.

22 Mar 1803, Joseph Cissna died on the River Rouge.

20 July 1807, Rebeca Cissne, 341.30 acres in Springwells, claim #28 of French Farms in Detroit Area:

Oct 1800, Joseph Cissne, Esq gave testimony in court about contested Election.

Dec 1802, James Cissne was a constable for Detroit.

1797, Joseph Cissne was Justice of Peace for River Rouge area.

9 July 1805, Jean Cissne was captain in the militia for Detroit.

20 Mar 1802, petition to governor for erection of Michigan Territory: signatories are Wiliam Cissne, James Cissne, Stephen Cisne and John Cissne. (Stephen lived in Chillicothe next to Governor)

22 March 1803, estate of Joseph Cissne stated that children of his first marriage are John, William, Sarah Corbus, and James. Children relinquished their claims because they have received inheritance from father during his lifetime.

Godfrey Corbus   married 1794
    Sarah Cissna-Corbus,   65/100
    Joseph C. Corbus, bn 1795   /100
    Richard W. Corbus, bn 1797   /100
    John Corbus, bn 1799   /100
    James G. Corbus, bn 1801   /100

William Cissna, bn 1773 <Joseph<John<the Frenchman   65/100
    Johanna Dicks-Cissna, bn ca 1778 (married 25 Dec 1798)
    Anna Cissna, bn 8 Mar 1779
    John Cissna, bn 16 Feb 1800   /101

    1 Oct 1805, Detroit tax list: William Cissna, 1 male, tax $1.00
    15 July 1796, First US Census taken after British surrender Detroit and
            Michigan Territory. Joseph Cisanney, James Cisanney, William
            Cissanney.
    French Farms in Detroit Area:
            20 July 1807, Wm. Cissne,   337.6 acres on Ecorce
    1812, List of First land owners of Wayne County, MI
        William Cissne on River Rouge, 337.6 acres, Claim #35
        William Cissna (Widow and Heirs) 293.32, Claim #665
    20 March 1803, Petition for Erection of Michigan Territory included the
            names William Cissne, James Cissne, Stephen Cissne,
            John Cissne
    15 Jan 1799, Election roll of Detroit listed William Cisney and Joseph
            Cisney
    25 Dec 1798, William Cissna married Johanna Dicks in Wayne County.
            Children; Sara bn 1801, Jane, John bn 1799, William bn 1804.
    6 Jan 1814, Brother James was appointed guardian of Sarah and William
            who are minors.

John Cissna, bn 1774 <Joseph<John<the Frenchman   66/107
    Jane Glass-Cissna, (will marry 12 Feb 1801)   /107

    10 May 1803, John Cissne was an ensign in Detroit Militia.
    1 Oct 1805, Detroit tax list: John Cissne, 1 male, 1 dog, tax $1.50
    1812, list of First land owners of Wayne County, MI
            John Cissne on River Rouge, 640 acres, Claim #31
            John Cissne on River Rouge, 351.6 acres, Claim #660

James Cissna, bn 1776 <Joseph<John<the Frenchman   66/107
    Elizabeth Cessna, bn 30 Dec 1779   /107
            <James<John<the Frenchman
    Jane Cissna, *will be born ca 1803*   /107
    Joseph Cissna, *will be born ca 1808*   /107

    15 July 1796, First US Census taken after British surrender Detroit and
            Michigan Territory. Joseph Cisanney, James Cisanney, William
            Cissanney.
    20 July 1807, James Cissne, 277.60 acres in Springwells

1812, list of First land owners of Wayne County, MI
> James Cissne on River Rouge, 144.65 acres, Claim #41

20 Mar 1803, Petition for Erection of Michigan Territory included the
> names William Cissne, James Cissne, Stephen Cissne,
> John Cissne

1800 North Carolina

1800 Buncombe County
Hot Springs

John Cessna Jr, bn 1780   <John Sr<**unknown**<the Frenchman   62/105
    Elizabeth Neilson-Cessna, bn ca 1780   /105

7 Sep 1798, John Cessna married Elizabeth Neilson in Greene
> County, TN, near to Hot Springs on the French Broad River.

10 Dec 1813, John Cessna Jr. and Elizabeth purchased 54 acres of
> John Strother's original land, located directly across the French
> Broad River from his father. Green Kennedy Cessna would have
> been born on this farm.

John Cessna Sr. bn   <Charles<John<the Frenchman
    John Cessna Sr, bn 1763   62/104
    Mary Cessna, bn ca 1764   62/104
    Male 16-26   *son-in-law*, bn ca 1784
    Female 16-26 *Daughter of John,* bn ca 1774   /104
    Male 10-16 *G-son of John,* bn 1794-1800   /104
    Male 10-16 *G-son of John,* bn 1794-1800   /104
    Female 10-16 *G-daughter of John,* bn 1794-1800   /104
    Female 10-16 *G-daughter of John,* bn 1794-1800
    Female 10-16 *G-daughter of John,* bn 1794-1800

2 May 1800, John Cessna, Sr purchased 120 on the French Broad River,
> The deed from John Strother dated described the farm as
> follows: John Strother was a land speculator who rented parcels
> of his land to people, and later sold them the same. This farm is
> just a few hundred yards from the border with Tennessee.

These individuals are extrapolated from 1810 Census. 1810 census of
> Buncombe County: Bean Twp (page 276 of Census). They
> evidently do not have the same last name, so they are children
> of a daughter.

Strongly suspect that this John was sheriff in both Bedford County, PA and Greene County, GA; and is a son of Col. Charles.

1800 Guilford County

John Sisney bn ca 1775 <Stephen<John<Stephen<the Frenchman   63/
       Wife of John, bn ca 1780

Stephen Sisney, bn ca 1745 <John<Stephen<the Frenchman   66/98
       Dolly Sisney, bn ca 1760   66/98
       Robert Sisney, bn ca 1784   66/98
       Mary Sisney, bn ca 1785   66/98
       Elizabeth Sisney, bn ca 1782   66/97
       Stephen William Sisney   66/98
       John "Scot" Sisney   66/98

1803-1805, Stephen and Dolly moved from NC to Christian County, KY and established a farm along Pond River. With them came a grandson, William Stephen Sisney.

John Taylor
       Rachel Sisney-Taylor, bn ca 1772   67/
          <Stephen<John<Stephen<the Frenchman
1798, Rachel Sisney married John Taylor in Greensboro, NC about 1778. Their first child, John Jr, was born ca 1799.

1800 Ohio

1800 Fairfield County

Thomas Cissna,   <Evans<John<the Frenchman   69/106
    Margaret Cissna, bn ca 1764   /106
    Robert Cissna, bn 1800   /106

Sep 1801, Governor St. Clair appointed Thomas Cesnau to be surveyor of Fairfield County.
1 Feb 1802, Thomas Cissna purchased public land 20 acres W ½ of section 15, Township18 for $640.
10 Dec 1804, Thomas Cissna purchased land from Barnabus McCarran. Both are from Butler Co.
1806, Thomas Cisna paid tax in Fairfield County
9 Jul 1804, Letters waiting at Chillicothe PO Thomas Cissna

1806 Fairfield County

Robert Cessna, bn 1785   69/106
    <Evans<John<The Frenchman

"As early as 1806 there were regular preaching places in Huntington. It is stated that probably Thomas and Robert Sisseney held the first meeting for prayer, and their houses were among the earliest of preaching places. Not only so, but they both on occasion could and would exhort".

1800 Ross County
Chillicothe

Stephen Cissna, bn 1755   68/108
    <Thomas<Stephen<the Frenchman
    Margaret Cissna, bn ca 1770   /108
    William Cissna, bn 1781   68/108
    Mary "Polly" Cissna, bn 1783   68/109
    James Cissna, bn ca 1789   68/108
    Elizabeth Cissna, bn ca 1785   68/104
    George Cissna, bn ca 1787   68/104

Stephen Cissna, bn ca 1794   /104
Malinda Cissna, bn ca 1798   /106
Eleanor Cissna, bn ca 1799   /104
Baldwin Cissna, born 28 Oct 1807   /104

20 Oct 1795, at Territorial Legislature in Cincinnati, Stephen Cisna was
    mentioned in discussions about building a ferry across the Great
    Miami River.
4 Mar 1799, Stephen Cisna served on a Jury in Chillicothe.
24 Dec 1799 Stephen Cissna and others got drunk and hung Governor St.
    Clair in effigy outside his hotel in Chillicothe. Series of news
    stories about this in weeks following.
1799 Stephen Cissna and Thomas Cissna are called as Witness for a case
    involving a debt in Chillicothe.
1800 Stephen Cissna called as a witness in a case involving debt.
1801 Stephen Cissna, Mrs. Cissna, Negro Dolly and others called as
    witnesses in US vs Meeker, on charge of violence.
June 1792, Stephen Cissna was a tavern keeper in Pittsburgh.
3 Sept 1793, Stephen Cisney and wife Margaret sold ½ of lot 202 in
    Pittsburgh for 50£.
23 Feb 1796, James Morrison of KY, using power of attny for Stephen
    Cisnay, sold lot #223 and all houses in Pittsburgh to Ebenezer
    Finnamore for 165£. Stephen Cissna was not present, but
    Margaret made her mark. (Title showed that Evan Cissna
    bought this lot from John Smith for 13£ on 1 Sep 1785)

John Cissna, bn 1779   68/107
              <Stephen<Thomas<Stephen<the Frenchman
    Elizabeth Moore-Cissna, bn ca 1781   /107
    Robert Cissna, bn 30 Apr 1800   /107

10 July 1802, Letters waiting at Chillicothe PO, John Cissna
15 Oct 1808, Benjamin Armstrong was sued by John Scissna.

Charles Cissna   <Stephen<Thomas<Stephen<Frenchman   68/
Samuel Cissna <Evans<John<the Frenchman   69/
    Charles and Samuel are apprentice Tailors in Pittsburgh in
    1800 but move to Chillicothe early in 1801.

18 June 1801, Charles Cissna was victim of assault by John Fennimore
18 June 1801, Charles Cissna was charged with assaulting John
    Fennimore (Fennimore becomes his bro-in-law).
18 June 1801, Charles Cissna and John Finnemore are convicted of
    assaulting each other in Chillicothe
1 Feb 1802, 160 acres sold to Cisna, Duncan & Ewing
12 Nov 1804, 559.66 acres sold to Cesna and Duncan

Letters waiting at Chillicothe PO, Samuel Cissna 16 Apr 1801,
Charles Cisney, 9 Jan 1802, Mary Fenimore 9 Apr 1807

Joseph Cissna, bn 1730   <**Unknown**<the Frenchman   /109
    Joseph Cissna Jr, bn ca 1774   /109
      Wife of Joseph Jr, bn ca 1780   /109
    Evans Cissna, bn ca 1780   /109
    David Cissna, bn ca 1790   /109
    Melinda Cissna, bn ca 1787   /109
    Daughter, bn ca 1789   /109

Extrapolated from 1810 Census.

1800 Pennsylvania

1800 Allegheny County
Pittsburgh

Evans Cissna   02001-00001-00   <John<the Frenchman
    Capt. Evans Cissna, bn 1728   69/
    Mary Cissna, bn 1755   69/
    Robert Cissna, bn 1787   69/105
    Samuel Cissna, bn 1781   69/108

Evans & Mary over 45. 2 sons 10-15. Robert later was reported as
    runaway.
20 Aug 1796, List of causes set down for Sept Term…Evans Cissna Vs
    Rt. Sitenberger
Sept 1797, Court Docket: Evans Cissna vs Archibald. C., Read U &
    wife Elizabeth
Sept 1797,   John Curry vs Mary Deery & Evan Cissna
1802, Court Docket Thomas Taylor vs Evans Cessney
1802-1807, Court Docket Wm. Gray vs Evan Cepney
2 June 1795,   Evan Cisna who sued as well as for himself as for the
    overseers of the poor of Mifflin Twp, Allegheny County, vs
    Thomas Tidball.
    1799, Evans Ciffna was one of dozens of people signing a petition in
    support of James Ross

Dec 1799, Jonathan Cochran vs Evan Cissna and Thomas Knowles
vs Evan Cissna et all

8 May 1802, "There will be a Sheriff's sale at the court House in the
Borough of Pittsburgh on Saturday, 8 May; 300 acres on Pine
creek, held in joint tenancy with Evan Cisna, seized and taken
in execution as the property of Emanuel Hoover, Jr at the suit of
Jeremiah Barker." Same property was listed again for sale on
Monday, 27 Sept 1802.

1 Dec 1802, List of Inhabitants of Pittsburgh on: Evan Cissna

2 Dec 1800, Census of Pittsburgh told each person's
occupation. Evan Cisna, Constable; Samuel and Charles Cissna
are tailors.

Theophilus Cisna   \<Stephen\<the Frenchman

Theophilus, bn 1730	75/106
Mary Cisna, bn ca 1740	75/106
wife of Theophilus	
James Cisna, bn ca 1785	75/106
William\<Theophilus\<Stephen\<the Frenchman	
Margaret, wife of James, bn ca 1783	/106

2 Dec 1800, Census of Pittsburgh told each person's occupation.
Evan Cisna, Constable; Theophales Cisna, Blue Dyer; John
Cisna, Taylor; Samuel Cisna, Taylor; Charles Cisna, Taylor

John Cissna   \<Evans\<John\<the Frenchman

John Cissna, bn ca 1780	69/110
\<Evans\<Charles\<the Frenchman	
wife of John Cissna, bn ca 1780	/110
John Cissna Jr, bn ca 1799	/110
Charles Cissna,	68/109
\<Stephen\<Thomas\<Stephen\<Frenchman	

1800 Census of Allegheny County
Page 51 John Sisna BP twp.; 1 male under 10, 2 males
16-26, 1 female 16-26

2 Dec 1800, Census of Pittsburgh told each person's occupation.
Evan Cisna, Constable; Theophales Cisna, Blue Dyer; John
Cisna, Taylor; Samuel Cisna, Taylor; Charles Cisna, Taylor

18 Dec 1807, "On this day, very early in the morning, John Cissney rode away on a light chesnut coloured mare, my property, as I have strong reason to believe with felonious intent…The said Cissney is short and stout, pock-marked, one of his eye-lids drawn rather down; had on a dark coat and corded overalls, the colour not particularly recollected. Whoever delivers the said mare to Robert Elrod at James Herron's (tavern-keeper) at McKee's Port, or to Thomas Cannon, Pittsburgh shall receive $10 reward and reasonable charges."

1800 Bedford County
1800 Colerain Twp

John Cessna Jr, bn 8 Dec 1764   70/111
<John<John<John<The Frenchman
Mary McCauslin-Cessna, bn 2 Mar1768   70/111
John Cessna, bn Feb 1787   70/111
Sarah "Sally" Cessna, bn 6 May 1788   70/111
Margaret Cessna, bn 6 Sep 1789   70/111
Mary Cessna, bn 2 Aug 1791   /111
John Cessna, bn Apr 1793   /111
Elizabeth Cessna, bn 17 Jan 1795   /111
Rachel Cessna, bn 7 Feb 1797   /111
William Cessna, 11 Jan 1799   /111
Samuel Cessna, bn 15 Oct 1800   /111

1797, John Cessna Jr. inherited the family homestead in Rainsburg, and
          moved from the Cumberland Valley farm back to Colerain farm.
21 June 1794, John Cessna Sr. applied for 400 acres in Bedford County
21 June 1794, John Cessna Jr applied for 400 acres in Bedford County

1800 Cumberland Valley Twp

Major John Cessna, bn 1726   <John<The Frenchman   69/
    Elizabeth Hall-Cessna, bn 1770   69/
    Charles Cessna, bn 10 Mar 1789   69/110
    Sarah Rose Cessna, bn 1791   69/110
    Evans Cessna, bn 2 Oct 1792   69/107
    Henry Cessna, bn 1791   69/110
    James Cessna, bn 22 Oct 1797   69/110
    Robert Hall (brother of Elizabeth), bn ca 1773

28 Feb 1804. Orphan's Court. Guardians appointed for Evans, James,
    Sarah & Henry Cissna children under age 14 of John Cessna,
    Esq, dec'd.
8 Mar 1802   Will of John Cessna, Sr. late of Bedford Twp. Tract of land
    purchased of Jacob Holtz to be divide among sons Charles,
    Evan, James & Henry. Daughter Sarah Rose Cessna to get
    moveable estate. Executors are sons John and Jonathan Cessna
    and Henry Williams.

William Cessna   <Major John<John<the Frenchman
    William Cessna, bn 20 June 1775   69/114
    Nancy Ann Barnes/Cessna, bn 8 Feb 1779   /114

1800 Census CV and Londonderry Twp, Bedford
    William Cessna: 1 male 16-25/ 1 female 16-25
1800 Taxables in Cumberland Valley Twp: William Cessna, single
    Freeman
1798 Pennsylvania, US Direct Tax Lists: John Hendrickson is occupant
    of a farm owned by William Cessna, in Cumberland Valley
    Twp; 1 house valued at $8; 50 acres, valued at $30.
1798 Pennsylvania, US Direct Tax Lists: Michael Boor is occupant
    of a farm owned by William Cessna in Cumberland Valley Twp;
    1 house valued at $8; 60 acres valued at $80

Henry Williams   71/
    Rebecca Cessna-Williams, 1 Aug 1762   71/113
        <John<John<Frenchman
    Hannah Williams,   24 May 1782   72/113
    John Williams,   30 Aug 1784   72/113
    Sarah "Sally" Williams, 1 Jul 1786   72/113
    Margaret P. Williams, 25 Feb 1789   72/113

Elizabeth Williams, 12 Apr 1791 /113
Rebecca Williams, 4 Mar 1794 /113
Rachael Williams, 9 Apr 1797 /113
Mary Williams, 11 Mar 1800 /113
Eleanor "Nellie" Williams, 6 Oct 1802 /113

21 June 1794, Rebecca Cessna applied for 400 acres in Bedford County
Her husband, Henry Williams died 1815

Charles Cessna, bn 1762   <William<John<the Frenchman   73/113
    Rachel Culbertson, bn ca 1764   /113
      (per daughter's gravestone) Married ca 1786
    William Franklin Cessna, bn ca 1786   /113
    Rachel Cessna, born 1793   /113
    Rebecca Cessna, bn ca 1790   /113
    Maria Cessna, bn ca 1795   /113
    Mary Ann Cessna, (died unmarried)

21 June 1794, Charles Cissna made a claim of 400 acres in Bedford
    County. Land is adjacent to that of Rachel Cessna. Family
    history reports he moved to Bedford County at that time.

Jonathan Cessna<Major John<John<the Frenchman   71/113
    Jonathan Cessna Sr, bn 16 Nov 1760   71/113
    Rebecca Worley-Cessna, 16-Aug-1764   71/113
    William Cessna, bn 29 Oct 1797   /113
    Jonathan Cessna Jr, bn 1 Apr 1789   71/113
    Stephen Cessna, bn 17 Apr 1782   71/112
    Charles Cessna, bn 8 Feb 1784   71/105
    Rachel Cessna, bn 1 June 1785   71/113
    Sarah Cessna, bn 18 Nov 1786   71/113
    John Cessna Sr, bn 26 Aug 1780   71/111
    Mary Ann McVicker, bn 31 Jan 1783   /111
      (Wife of son John)

It appears that son Ezekiel Cessna, bn 12 May 1791 and daughter,
    Margaret Cessna, bn 23 Dec 1792 died before 1800.
16 June 1794, Jonathan Cessna warranted 400 acres in Bedford County
21 June 1794, Jonathan Cessna Jr warrant 400 acres in Bedford County
1798 Pennsylvania, US Direct Tax Lists: Jonathan Cessna was owner
    of farm in Cumberland Valley Twp; 1 house valued at $58;
    340 acres valued at $1000.

1800 Taxables showed Jonathan Cessna in Cumberland Valley Twp
1800 Census Bedford County   Colerain Twp
    Jonathan Cessna: 1 male under 10, 1 male 10-16, 2 males 16-25,
        1 male 26-45; 1 female under 10, 1 female 10-16, 1 female
        16-26, 1 female 26-45

1800 Bedford Boro

William J. Vickory, bn 1768
        Elizabeth Cessna, bn 1768   69/114
            <John<John<The Frenchman
        Mary Cessna Vickory, bn 1796   /114
        John Cessna Vickory, bn 1708   /114
        William T. Vickory, bn 1800   /114

1795, Elizabeth Cessna married William Vickory.

1800 Cumberland County
1800 Shippensburg Twp

James Cisna, bn 1751   <John<the Frenchman   72/115
        Mary ?-Cessna, bn ca 1757 wife of James   72/115
        James Cessna, bn 1784   72/115
        William Cissna, bn ca 1777   72/115
        John Cessna, bn 30 Dec 1779   72/115
        James Cessna, bn Apr 1751   72/115
        Sarah Cessna, bn ca 1788   72/115
        Margaret Cessna, bn ca 1789   72/115
        Mary Cessna, bn ca 1786   72/113

1793 Census of Cumberland County, PA Shippensburg, James Sisna
15 Nov 1797, James Cessna advertised "for sale house on lot #79 in
        Shippensburg, which has long been used as a tavern." There is
        no land record of James owning this property.
1800 taxables for Shippensburg, Cumberland County James Cisna,
        farmer; William Cisna, farmer; John Cisna, Tanner.
17 Feb 1810, James Cessna advertised for sale, land purchased from John
        Penn was next to John Cessna's land in South Hampton Twp.

1793 Direct Tax, 3rd Assessment District, 4th Division
  James Cisna, lot on King Street, neighbor was John Simpson
1793 Direct Tax, 3rd Assessment District, 6th Division
  James Cissna, resident/owner, 1 Smith Shop 20'20', on King
  Street, John Simpson neighbor, James Cissna, resident/owner, 1
  Smith Shop 20'20', Sam Tate & Wm McKnight neighbors
1793 Direct Tax, 3rd Assessment District, 5th Division
  James Cissna 1 house, 22'x24', tax 2.9.123
     1 Kitchen, 16'x16'
     1 Stable, 18'x20
1798 Direct Tax, 3rd Assessment District, 6th Division
  James Cissna owner, Southampton House & lot, 22'x24' wood,
  $850.00 value. James Cissna owner, Samuel Tate resident,
  kitchen 16'x16', Wood, $2112.00 value. James Cissna owner,
  William McKnight resident, stable 18'x20', wood
1798, James Cissna paid tax on Lot King St. of 61p on value of 50£.
  John Simpson is his neighbor.
1799 Shippensburgh Tax
  James Cisney, 2 houses, 3 lots, $350
1802 Shippensburgh Twp Tax, Cumberland County
  James Cesney, 1 house, 2 lots, 2 horses, 3 cows, $783

1800 Toboyne Twp

Stephen Cisney, bn 28 Dec 1766   71/115
   <Maj John<John<the Frenchman
Mary Gardner-Cisna, bn ca 1768   /115
  married 12 April 1790
John Cisna, bn ca 1791   /115
Male under 10 (unknown Son)   /115
Stephen Cisna Jr. bn 1790-1800   /115
Stephen Cisna, bn 28 Dec 1766   /115
Elizabeth Cisna, bn 1796   /115
Julia Cisna, bn 1798   /115

Info comes from House of Cessna, but did not mention any sons who
  died before 1810.
1793 Census of Toboyne Twp, Cumberland County PA, Stephen Sisna
12 Apr 1790, Stephen Cisney of Bedford marries Mary Gardner of
  Centre, in Perry County
11 Sept 1793, Mary Cisne bought land from John Gardner Sr in Toboyne
3 Jan 1797, Stephen Cisney bought land from Jno. Gardner Sr in Toboyne

12 June 1795, Stephen Cessna purchased 50 acres in Cumberland County
from the government

1800 taxables for Toboyne Twp Cumberland County Stephen Cisna Jr,
T. Keep

*The unknown boys might be in-laws, or sons who are not recorded in
House of Cessna.

1793 Tax Toboyne Twp Cumberland County
Stephen Cisna, 2 horses, 1 cow, $11.10
(1789 F-I-L John Gardner Sr had 125 acres, 2 horse, 3 cow)

1795 Tax Toboyne Twp Cumberland County
Stephen Cesna, 2 horses, 2 cows, $40

1799 Tax Toboyne Twp Cumberland County
Stephen Cisna 49 acres, $294: 96 acres Ridge Land, $144
2 horse, 2 cows, $96   Total $534

1802 Tax Toboyne Twp Cumberland County
Stephen Cessna, 46 acres, $368:76 acres Ridge land, $60
2 horses, 2 cows, $84,   total $51

1805 Tax Toboyne Twp Cumberland County
Stephen Cisna, 51 acres, $408; 50 acres Ridge Land, $100
3 horses $120, 2 Cows $16,   total $644

1808 Tax Toboyne Twp Cumberland County
Stephen Cissna, 50 ac land, $500; 50 ac ridge land, $100
3 horses, $120; 3 cows, $23; Total $744

1800 US Census of Toboyne Twp: Stephen Cisney and wife are 26-45;
3 boys under 10, 2 girls under 10.

1800 Franklin County
1800 Fannet Township

Thomas Cissna, bn 1760   <Theophilus<Stephen<the Frenchman   75/117
   Mrs. -Cisna, bn ca 1760   75/117
   Thomas Henderson Cisna, bn 1778   75/117
   Archibald Cisna, bn ca 1780   75/117
   Theophilus J. Cisna, bn ca 1782   75/117
   John Alfred Cisna, bn ca 1785   75/117
   William Henry Cisna, bn ca 1787   75/117
   David Alexander Cisna, bn ca 1789   75/117

1798, In Franklin County, Fannet Twp: description of houses; Thos Cisna
rented home, own by Heirs of Wm. McIntire, 20x22 log
house, 2 stories, 3 windows, 36 lights, on 2 acres of land,
vallued at $300. (lights means panes of glass).
Names provided by House of Cessna, but not dates.

Stephen Sisney bn ca 1767   75/116
        <Theophilus<Stephen<the Frenchman
    Theophilus Cisna, bn ca 1785   75/116
        <Stephen<Theophilus<Stephen<the Frenchman
    Wife of Theophilus, bn 1775-85   75/116

Theophilus Cisna, bn 1760   <John<the Frenchman   75/117
    Nancy Richardson-Cisna, bn ca 1770   75 /117
    Betsey Cisna, bn ca 1797   75/117
    Martha "Agnes" Cisna, bn ca 1796   /117
    Stephen Cisna, bn ca 1799   /117
    James Cisna, bn ca 1794   75/117

    25 Sept 1799, Theophilus Cisna married Nancy Richardson; performed
        by David Denny in Chambersburg, PA
    1800 Taxables Fannettsburg, Franklin, PA Theophilus Cisna

William Cissna bn 1764 <Theophilus<Stephen<the Frenchman   74/117
    Wife of William bn, ca 1768   74/117
    James Cisna, bn ca 1788   74/117
    George Cisna, bn ca1790   74/117

    About 1808, William, wife and George migrated down the Great
       Wagon Road to Pleasantburg, South Carolina: soon to become
       Greenville.
       Names provided by House of Cessna, but not dates.

Margaret Cissna   widow of Stephen Cissna
        <Theophilus<Stephen<the Frenchman
    Margaret ?-Cissna, bn 1776-1784   75/117
    Theophilus Cisna, bn 1790-1800   75/117
    Daughter, bn 1790-1800   /117

    Stephen Cisna was born about 1767 and died between 1797-1800
    10 Feb 1797, Lt Stephen Cessna, 4th company, 1st Regiment of
       Cumberland County Militia, return of election of
       officers. Hopewell Twp, Cumberland County
    1800 Fannettsburg, Franklin cty, PA Margaret Cisney 1 male under 10,
       1 female under 10, 1 female 16-25

James Cisna, bn ca 1782 <Theophilus<Stephen<the Frenchman   75/117
    Wife of James, bn ca 1781   /117
    Washington Cisna, bn ca 1798   /117
    Thomas Cisna, bn ca 1800   /117

Names provided by House of Cessna but not dates.

1800 Huntington County
Dublin Twp

Theophilus Sisney
        <Thomas<Theophilus<Stephen<the Frenchman
    Theophilus Sisney, bn ca 1780   76/115
    Margaret McGuire-Sisney, bn ca 1780   /115

1810 Census

1810 Georgia

1810 Morgan County

John Royston
>> **Polly Baker-Cessna-Royston,** bn ca 1765   77/
>> **Samuel Cessna,** bn 1790   77/117
>>> \<Samuel\<Charles\<the Frenchman
>> **Elizabeth Cessna,** bn 1787   77/117
>>> \<Samuel\<Charles\<the Frenchman

> 6 Jan 1803, Polly (widow of Samuel) married John Royston.

Robert Baker Cessna, bn 1784   77/117
>> \<Samuel\<Charles\<the Frenchman
> **Wife,** bn ca 1783   /117
> **Robert Cessna,** bn 1803   /117

> Robert's wife died after one child.

1810 Kentucky

1810 Christian County
Farm On Pond River

Robert Sisney,
>> **Robert Cisney,** bn ca 1788   79/123
>>> \<Stephen\<John\<Stephen\<the Frenchman

Mary Gatting-Cessna, bn ca 1790 /123

Female, bn 1810 who did not survive /123

George Washington Cisney bn 1803 /123

Benjamin Franklin "Frank" Cisney bn 1802 /123
> <unknown<John<Stephen<the Frenchman
> History of Christian County states Frank Cisney was an orphan raised by his uncle.

5 Dec 1815, Luther Calvin married Peggy Gaylord; with Rev. Robert Sisney presiding ceremony.

1814, Hopkins County, Robert Chisney was indicted for assault on William Bird. About same time: Robert Chisney was named road Surveyor.

Stevin Sisney bn 1745

    Stephen Sisney, 84/123
> <John<Stephen<the Frenchman

    Dolly Holten-Sisney, bn ca 1760 84/123

    Elizabeth Sisney, bn 1785 /120

    Stephen William Sisney, bn 1794 84/124
> <Stephen<John<Stephen<the Frenchman

    John "Scot" Sisney<Stephen<John<Stephen<the Frenchman 84/124

48 April 1807, 175 acres surveyed and entered for Stephen Cisney on Pond River Course in Christian County.

15 July 1816, Stephen Sisney married Betsy Troyver in Christian County. Stephen Sisney and Mrs. Brown secure bonds for the marriage.

1810 Hardin County

William Cessna, bn 17 June 1776 77/124
> <Jonathan<John<the Frenchman

    Sarah "Sally" Wallace-Cessna bn ca 1780 /124

    Jonathan Friend Cessna, bn 16 Nov 1806 /124

    Mary Cessna, bn ca 1802 /124

    Daughter, bn ca 1804 /124

    Elizabeth "Betsey" Cessna, bn ca 1806 /124

    Mary Friend-Cessna, bn ca 1755 77/
> Widow of Jonanthan Cessna<John<the Frenchman

12 April 1802, William W. Cessna married Sarah Wallace in Hardin County, KY.

1803, Margaret Cessna died in infancy.

Sheperd Gum
Nancy Agnes Cessna-Gum,   77/125
bn ca 1774 <Jonathan<John<the Frenchman

1810 Muhlenberg County

Robert Cessna, bn 1775 <Charles<Charles<the Frenchman   78/
     Elizabeth Culbertson-Cessna, bn ca 1780   78/125
     Elizabeth Cessna, bn 1795   78/125
     Mary E. Cessna, bn ca 1798   78/125
     Nancy Cessna, bn 16 Mar 1801   /125
     Johanna L. Cessna, bn 2 Feb 1803   /125
     Margaret "Peggy" D. Cessna, bn ca 1805   /125
     Charles Cessna, bn ca 1806   /125
     Sarah "Sally" Culbertson Cessna, bn 1808   /125
     Robert John Culberson Cessna, born 7 Apr 1814

22 Apr 1805, Robert Cessna paid tax on 200 acres on Green River.
28 Jul 1806, Robert Cessna, John Culbertson, Joseph Culbertson and Sam
      Long were appointed to lay out a road from Wm. McCommon's
      fence to the road at Martin's Ferry on the Green River.
20 Apr 1807, The road from Culbertson's Ford to Greenville to go past
      the fence of Robert Cessna.
11 Jul 1814, Elizabeth Cessna, widow of Robert Cessna, appointed to
      be administrator of his estate. Bond posted by James Milligan,
      James Sharp and Robert Glenn.

James Milligan
     Elizabeth Cessna-Milligan, bn ca 1766   79/122
        <Charles<John<the Frenchman
     John C Milligan, bn 20 Dec 1789   79/122
     Melia Milligan, bn 22 Mar 1792   79/122
     Melinda Milligan, bn 1 Jul 1795   79/122
     Charles Milligan, bn 20 Jan 1800   79/122
     James Milligan, bn 1802

8-19-1788, Elizabeth Cessna married James Milligan in Green County,
      GA

1803, the Milligans did go with Charles to Mississippi. About 1806
Elizabeth died there. James returned to Muhlenberg County
and remarried in 1807; having four more children.

James Sharp

Sarah "Sally" Sharp, bn 1780	79/126
<William<William<John<Frenchman	
Robert Cessna Sharp, bn 7 Oct 1804	/126
Samuel Cessna Sharp, bn 26 Jan 1803	/126
William McCormic Shrp, bn 22 Feb 1806	/126
Charles Culbertson Sharp, bn 22 Ap 1808	/126
John Nelson Sharp, bn1811	/126
Son, bn ca 1813	
1 Slave	

Apr 1802, Sarah "Sally" Cessna married James Sharp in Muhlenberg
County.
Note: Family records only list 5 sons for James and Sally.

1810 Michigan

1810 Wayne County

Sarah Cissna-Corbus, bn 1782 <Joseph<John<the Frenchman	81/127
Richard W. Corbus, bn ca 1805	81/127
Joseph Cissna Corbus, bn ca 1802	81/127
John Corbus, bn ca 1804	81/127
James Corbus, bn ca 1806	81/127

1807, Godfrey Corbus died. She later married John Macomb.
Sarah was instrumental in establishing the Methodist Church in
Detroit, and during War of 1812 she led the church in efforts to
assist refugees of the war.

William Cissna bn 1773 <Joseph<John<the Frenchman	81/
Hanna Dicks-Cissna, bn ca 1781	81/128
Jane (Jeanne) Cissna, bn 1803	/123

Sara "Sally" Cissna, bn 1801   /128
William Cissna, bn 1804   /128
John Cissna, bn 1799   78/128

Dec 1811, William was one of the first victims of Tecumseh's War which
    opened the War of 1812.
1812, Hannah Dicks-Cissne (widow of William) marries John Burbank.
    Hannah died 2 April 1813, leaving Jane, Sally, William and
    John. James Cissne is appointed administrator. Hiram Johns
    married Jane.
6 Jan 1814, William's brother, James, was appointed guardian of Sarah
    and William who are minors on. Jane married and stayed in MI.
    His son, John, moved to Holmes County, OH with Uncle James.

Stephen P. Cissna, bn 1785   81/121
        <Joseph<John<the Frenchman
Mary Moore-Cissna, bn ca 1790   /121
Amanda Jane Cissna, bn 1810   /121

10 June 1818, The town of Rockport Indiana was opened for settlement
    with a large auction selling most all of the town lots. Dr. Stephen
    P. Cissna moved his family there to open his practice.
    Mary died before 1820.

Joseph Cissna, bn 24 June 1789   <Joseph<John<the Frenchman   81/121

10 June 1818, The town of Rockport Indiana was opened for settlement
    with a large auction selling most all of the town lots.
    Joseph moved there with his brother's family. Their brother,
    David Cissna, served as an early Sheriff.

David M. Cissna   <Joseph<John<Frenchman   81/122

1810 Mississippi

1810 Jefferson County
Farm north of Utica, MS

Col Charles Cessna, bn 1724   <John<the Frenchman   78/
    William S. Cessna, bn ca 1790   78/129
        <Charles<John<the Frenchman
    Joseph (aka James?) Cessna, bn ca 1787   78/129
   75/125 < *unknown* <Charles<John<the Frenchman
    Culbertson D. Cessna, bn 19 Feb 1789   78/125
        < *unknown* <Charles<John<the Frenchman

25 Aug 1802, Petition to Congress, by citizens of territory asking that the land office be in the area, settlers on vacant land have a pre-emption right, & suffrage be for males of full age: Charles Cessna, William Cessna, James Milligan, Aaron Neel

4 Sept 1806, As the United States took control of the Mississippi Territory, a list of those people who have already settled there was presented to the US House of Representatives to have their land claims validated. Among them Charles Cissna for 271 acres James Milligan 438 acres; Aaron Neel 300 acres on Bayou Pierre Watershed and William Cissna for 160 acres; John Robinette 280 acres on River Homochitto watershed.

1805 Census of Jefferson County: Charles Cisney one wm +21 = Col Charles: 3 wm -21:   2 bf = slaves

1808 Mississippi Territorial Census, Jefferson County: Charles Cissna 3/1/0/0/0/4/0/5/9
    3 WM under 21; 1 WM over 21; No females; 4 total whites; 5 slaves;   total 9

1810 Census of Jefferson County: Charles Cisner....3/1/0/0/4

23 July 1811, Charles Cessna sold three horses, 18 head of horned cattle, 30 head of hogs and all his household furniture and farming utensils for $200 to Joseph, William and Culbertson Cessna. Aaron Neel and Elizabeth Robenett witness sale.

Note: G-son, Charles, got the plantation, but other boys get (buy?) their inheritance before he died.

1816 Census of Jefferson Cty, Charles Cissna 1 male over 21, 4 slaves. This would be Charles Cessna, g-son of Col. Charles.

.

Aaron Neel   1/5/1/1/0/8   80/129
    Aaron Neel, bn ca 1765
    Mary Cessna-Neel bn ca 1769   80/129

<Charles<John<the Frenchman

Charles Cessna Neel, bn 1795   80/128

Robert Cessna Neel, bn ca 1819   80/125

Thomas S. Neel, bn ca 1797   80/125

Aaron Lovett Neel, bn ca 1793   80/125

Charles Cessna, bn ca 1785   80/126
 <Charles<John<Frenchman

Elizabeth Neel, bn ca 1801   76/125

Caroline Neel, born soon after 1810 (married Gideon Tidwell)

Lurenna Smith Neel, born soon after 1810.

25 Aug 1802, Petition to Congress by citizens of territory asked that the land office be in the area, settlers on vacant land have a preemption right, & suffrage be for males of full age: Charles Cessna, William Cessna, James Milligan, Aaron Neel

4 Sept 1806, As the United States took control of the Mississippi Territory, a list of those people who have already settled there is present to the US House of Representatives to have their land claims validated. Among them is Charles Cissna for 271 acres; James Milligan 438 acres; Aaron Neel 300 acres on Bayou Pierre Watershed; and William Cissna for 160 acres; John Robinette 280 acres on River Homochitto watershed.

1808 Mississippi Territorial Census, Jefferson County:
 Aaron Neel 5/1/0/1/0/7/0/1/8
  5 WM under 21; 1 WM over 21; 0 WF under 21; 1 WF over 21;
   7 total White; 1 slave total 8

1810 Census of Jefferson County: Aaron Neel....1/5/1/1/0/8

320 Acres on River Homocito Water Shed

This land would eventually become Copiah and then Adams Counties.

William W. Cessna, bn 1768 1/3/1/0/0/5   74/129
 William Cessna, , bn 1768
  <William<John<the Frenchman

Margaret *Robinette*-Cessna, bn ca 1770   74/129

John Cessna, bn 1793   74/129

James Cessna, bn 1798   74/129

John Robinette, bn ca 1790   74/129

4 Sept 1806, As the United States took control of the Mississippi
Territory, a list of those people who have already settled there
is present to the US House of Representatives to have their land
claims validated. Among them was Charles Cissna for 271 acres;
James Milligan 438 acres; Aaron Neel 300 acres on Bayou
Pierre Watershed; **and** William Cissna for 160 acres; John
Robinette 280 acres on River Homochitto watershed.
1808 Mississippi Territorial Census, Jefferson County:
    William Cissna 3/2/0/1/0/6/0/2/8
    3 WM under 21; 2 WM over 21; 1 WF over 21; 6 Total white;
        2 slaves   total 8
    1816 Census of Mississippi
        Wm Cessna Sr, 7 males over 21, no females
        William Cissna Jr., 2 males over 21, 1 female

William W. Sisney Jr. <William<William<John<the Frenchman
    William Cessna Jr, bn 1795   79/
    Male over 21 _?_____

    15 Nov 1806, Certificate Entered:
        Certificate: 35   Certificate Date: 04 Sep 1806
        Claim Name: William Cissna Orig Name: William Cissna
        Quantity: 320 ac Situation: River Homochitto
    1810 Census of Jefferson County Mississippi Territory:
        William Sisney Jr /0/0/0/   2 males over 21...2 total whites
        William Cisna.....1/3/1/0/0/5
        1 male over 21; 3 males under; 1 female over; 3 slaves

1810 North Carolina

1810 Buncombe County

John Cessna Sr. bn   <Charles<John<the Frenchman
    John Cessna Sr, bn 1763   83/131
    Mary Cessna, bn ca 1764   83/
    son-in-law, bn ca 1784   83/
    Daughter of John, bn ca 1774   83/131
    G-son of John, bn ca 1805   83/131
    G-son of John, bn ca 1803   83/130
    G-son of John, bn 1794-1800   83/

G-son of John, bn 1794-1800   83/
G-daughter of John, bn 1800-1810   83/130
G-daughter of John, bn 1794-1800
G-daughter of John, bn 1794-1800
G-daughter of John, bn 1794-1800   /
8 slaves

> Note: This is a very large family. If they were all Cessnas, more would
>   show up in the next two census. The indication is that these
>   folks all have another surname, probably John Cessna's
>   daughter, husband and children. More Research is needed!

John Cessna Jr. bn ca 1770   <John<Charles<John<the Frenchman
     John Cessna Jr.   83/
     Elizabeth Nielson-Cessna, bn ca 1780   83/
     Green Kennedy Cessna, bn 1805   /126
     Son, born deaf and blind, 1800-1810   /126
     Daughter, born 1800-1810   /126
     10 Slaves

> In the book: Hot Springs of North Carolina, it was reported that John
>   Cessna who married Elizabeth Nielson had come up from
>   Natchez where he had a large and wealthy family there. This
>   detail would indicate that John Cessna in Buncombe County was
>   a part of Col. Charles Cessna family. John Cessna, brother of
>   Col.Charles, did have slaves as Sheriff of Greene Cty, GA.
> 1820 Census: Green K. Cessna was head of household and caring for deaf
>   and dumb brother.

1810 Ohio
1810 Coshocton County

Charles Cissna   <Jonathan<John<John<the Frenchman   91/131
     Anne ?-Cessna   wife of Charles   /131
     James O. Cessna   bn 1809   /131

Nancy Cisney, bn ca 1810   /131
1814 Tax list of Jackson Twp listed Charles Cissna as owning land in
    Range 8, Township 5, Section 17.

1810 Fairfield County

Thomas Cissna, bn 1778   <Evans<John<the Frenchman   85/
    Margaret Cissna, bn ca 1780   85/132
    Robert Cissna, bn 1800   85/132
    Eliza Cissna bn 1804-1810   /132
           <Thomas<Evans<Charles<the Frenchman
    Maria Cissna bn 1804-1810   /132
           <Thomas<Evans<Charles<the Frenchman
    Hannah Cissna/Rees/Paxton bn 1801-1804

           <Thomas<Evans<Charles<the Frenchman

24 Feb 1812, Thomas Cissna was a witness on a will made in Fairfield
    County by Ludwick Bousey.
Lancaster, OH, Thomas Cisna was an early inhabitant. He lived on the
    south side of Main, about midway between Fourth Street and
    Broad. In 1815 he was a farmer one mile west of town and a
    breeder of fine Merino sheep, which he announced in the Ohio
    Eagle. He died while on a trading voyage to New Orleans.

Robert Cissna, bn 1778   <Evans<John<the Frenchman   85/123
                                           or/102
8 Oct 1806, Ad in Scioto Gazette: "Robert Cisna, 17 years old, 5'5', an ill
    look & ungovernable temper. He was wearing a roundabout
    stripped cotton jacket, swandsdown waist coat, stripped
    pantaloons, fur hat and new shoes. Brand on left arm: R. Cis.
    Fled the apprentiship of E. Pentland in Pittsburg, PA. Is believed
    to have family in Chillicothe."
"As early as 1806 there were regular preaching places in Huntington. It is
    stated that probably Thomas and Robert Sisseney held the first
    meeting for prayer, and their houses were among the earliest of
    preaching places. Not only so, but they both on occasion could
    and would exhort."
After his brother Thomas' death on a trading trip to New Orleans, Robert
    relocated to western Missouri. Robert may have been along on
    trip to New Orleans.

1810 Holmes County

John Cissna, bn 1775   <Joseph<John<the Frenchman   82/140
    Jane Glass-Cissna, bn ca 1778   82/140
    Jonathan Alexander Cissna, bn 1802   /140
    Elizabeth Cissna, bn 13 Sept 1806   /140
    Joseph G. Cissna, bn 25 Feb 1809   /140

    1811, John and James Cissna came to the county in a dugout canoe and
        traded goods with the Indians.
    Aug 1811, John Cisna was associate Judge of Wayne County, OH.
        (Wooster). Later become Holmes County.
    27 Oct 1810, John Cissne bought 160 acres in Prairie Twp, Holmes
        County, OH.

James Cissna, bn 1776 <Joseph<John<the Frenchman   82/140
    Elizabeth Cessna-Cissna, bn 30 Dec 1779   82/140
        <James<John<the Frenchman
    Jane Cissna, born ca 1803   <James<Joseph<John<Frenchman   /140
    Joseph Cissna, born ca 1808 <James<Joseph<John<Frenchman   /136
    Margaret Cissna, bn 1812 <James<Joseph<John<Frenchman   /140
    Anne Cissna, bn 1799 <William<Joseph<John<Frenchman   82/140
    John Cissna, bn 1800 <William<Joseph<John<Frenchman   82/140
    Jane Cissna, bn 1803 <William<Joseph<John<Frenchman   /140
    Sarah Cissna, bn 1804   <William<Joseph<John<Frenchman   /140
    William Cissna, bn 1806   <William<Joseph<John<Frenchman   /140
    Jeanee Cisne, <William<Joseph<John<Frenchman   /127
    6 Nov 1810, James Cissne bought 160 acres in Prairie Twp, Holmes Cty,
        OH.
    1814, James became the legal guardian of the children of his brother,
        William who was killed by Indians in 1811 during Tecumseh's
        War at the beginning of the War of 1812

1810 Ross County

John Cissna, bn 1779   88/139
        <Stephen<Thomas<Stephen<the Frenchman
    Elizabeth Moore-Cissna, bn 1781   88/139
    Robert Cissna, bn 20 Apr 1800   88/139
    Elizabeth Cissna, bn 1802   /139

Jane Cissna, bn ca 1804 /139
Charles Cissna, bn 4 Dec 1808 /139
William M. Cissna, bn 1810 /139

1799, John Cessna and Elizabeth Moore married in Chillicothe.

Stephen Cissna bn 1755 <Thomas<Stephen<the Frenchman 85/137
    Margaret Hegan-Cissna, bn ca 1776 85/137
    William W. Cissna, bn ca 1781 85/137
    James Cissna, bn ca 1789 85/138
    Joseph Cissna, bn 1776 85/132
    Elizabeth Cissna, bn ca 1790 85/133
    George Cissna, bn ca 1791 85/133
    Stephen Cissna, bn 1794 85/137
    Malinda Cissna, bn 1798 85/138
    Eleanor Cissna, bn 1799 85/138
    Baldwin Cissna, bn 28 Oct 1807 85/133

31 Aug 1810, Stephen Cisna bought Chillicothe lot 149 (E half) from
    Jacob Poisal & wife for $500
1806, Stephen Cissna was an early hotel keeper in Chillicothe
20 May 1818, James Cissna married Catherine Ewing
4 Feb 1820, Eleanor Cissna married Samuel Porter in Chillicothe
20 June 1815, Melinda Cissna married Robert Chelfin
8 Sep 1820, Melinda married again to John Renshaw

Samuel Cissna, bn ca 1781, <Evans<John<the Frenchman 87/130
    Mary Wilcutt-Cissna, bn ca 1785 /130
    David Cissna, bn ca 1805 /130
    John Cissna, bn ca 1806 /130
    James Cissna, bn 1807 /130
    Charles Cissna, bn 1809 /130

1810 & 1818 Scioto Twp Tax lists: Charles Cisney & Samuel Cisney
1810-1811, Ross County Tax: Samuel Cissna 500, Ac, non-resident, $5
8 July 1803, Samuel Cissna bought Franklinton lot 174 from John May
    for $175
5 May 1802, Samuel Cissna bought Chillicothe lot 176 from Aaron
    Sullivan for $15

Charles Cissna, bn 12 Feb 1783   88/136
        <Stephen<Thomas<Stephen<the Frenchman
   Dorcus Wilcutt-Cissna, bn ca 1787   /136
   Evans Cissna, bn 1802   /136
   Mary H. B. Cissna, bn 1 July 1806   /136
   David Cissna, bn 4 Oct 1808   /136
   John B. Cissna, born 7 Nov 1810

1810 & 1818 Scioto Twp Tax: Charles Cisney & Samuel Cisney
1810-11 Ross County Tax List: Samuel Cissna 500 A, nonresident, $5
     Charles Cissna 97 ½ acres originally owned by George Gibbon,
     land near Indian Creek.
1813 Ross County Tax: Charles Cissna, 97 ½ acres "With the auditor",
     original proprieter was George Gibbons, Near Indian Creek.
     Charles pays back taxes for 1812 & 1813; $.63
14 June 1809, Charles Cissna bought Chillicothe lot 256 from John
     McDongal & wife for $700
15 June 1815, Charles Cissna bought Chillicothe lot 258 from
     John Sherer for $2500
26 July 1808, Charles Cissna at Chillicothe offered all his household
     furniture for sale as well as his house and lots.

Joseph Cissna, bn 1774   <**unknown**<the Frenchman   87/137
   Wife of Joseph Cissna (Ms Howe?), bn ca 1775   87/137
   Joseph P. Cissna, bn 1801   87/137
   David Cissna, bn ca 1805   87/137
   Melinda Cissna, bn ca 1795   87/137
   Evans Cissna, bn ca 1797   87/137

1809 Scioto Twp tax: Joseph Ceeney, 140 Ac square, adjoining
     Chillicothe on the Scioto River.
1809 Union Twp Tax: Joseph Cissna, 113 Ac, originally owned by
     Nathaniel Massie on Scioto River.
20 June 1815, Melinda Cissna married Robert Chelfin
1821, Joseph P. Cissna married Asenith Repose in Ross County.
1831, David moved to Spencer County, IN.
1838, David became Marshal of Spencer County, IN.
19 May 1817, Evans Cissna married Margaret McCrary in Ross County

Thomas Jones
   Mary "Polly" Cissna, bn ca 1784   85/
        <Stephen<Thomas<Stephen<the Frenchman
1 Man 1809, Polly Cessna married Thomas Jones in Ross County
     Thomas and Mary had five daughters before 1820.

1810 Pennsylvania

1810 Alleghany County
St. Clair Twp

Theo Scisney   <Stephen<the Frenchman
    Theophilus Cisna, bn ca 1720   88/142
    Sarah Cisna, bn ca 1740   88/

John Cissna bn 1780   <Evans<John<the Frenchman   88/
    John Cissna Jr. bn 1799   88/
    Wife of John Cissna bn ca 1780   88/

1810 Bedford County

George Cessna, bn ca 1780
    <**unknown**<John<the Frenchman

    9 Feb 1796, Michael Sill applied for 50 a, adjoining lands of Michael
        Feather on East, Conrad Samuel on the North & George Cessna
        on South. In Bedford Twp.

1810 Colerain Twp

Charles Cisney   <John<John<the Frenchman   90/111
    Kathyrn "Katie" Smouse-Cessna, bn ca 1789   /111

    1810 Census Colerain Twp, Bedford County
        Charles Cisney, 1 male under 10, 1 male 10-16, 1 male 16-26,
          1 female 16-26
    1814 Colerain Twp tax: Charles Cessna, 2 horses, 2 cows value $8,
        tax $1.04

John Cessna Jr, bn 8 Dec 1764   <John<John<the Frenchman   88/
    Mary McCauslin-Cessna, bn 2 Mar 1768   89/142
    John Cessna, bn Feb 1787 d Apr 1787   89/

Sarah "Sally" Cessna, bn 6 May 1788   89/140
Margaret Cessna, bn 6 Sep 1789 d 25 Sep 1806   89/
Mary Cessna, bn 2 Aug 1791 d 23 Sep 1806   89/143
John Cessna, bn Apr 1793 d Feb 1796   89/143
Elizabeth Cessna, bn 17 Jan 1795   89/149
Rachel Cessna, bn 7 Feb 1797   89/149
William Cessna, bn 11 Jan 1799   89/143
Samuel Cessna, bn 15 Oct 1800   89/139
John Cessna bn 4 Jul 1802 died 29 Sep 1806
Ellen Cessna, bn 6 May 1805   /142
Eleanor Cessna, bn 20 May 1807   /142

1802, John Cessna inherited the family farm from his father
        Maj. John Cessna.
5 Aug 1813, John Cessna died in Colerain Twp.
1825, Mary McCauslin Cessna died in Colerain Twp. 6 children
        preceeded her.

1810 Cumberland Valley Twp

Charles Sisney   <Jonathan<John<John<the Frenchman   91/127
    Charles Cessna, bn 8 Feb 1784   /127
    Anna ?-Cessna, bn ca 1789 wife of Charles   /127
        Daughter of Charles, bn 1800-1810   /127
    James O. Cessna, bn ca 1809
    Evans Cisney   /132

1814 Cumberland Valley Twp tax: Charles Cessna, 1 house, 5 horses,
        2 cattle, laborer $109,
1814, Charles Cessna and Nathan Wright came to Coshocton County
        from Perry Township in Bedford County, PA

John Sisney, bn 26 Aug 1780   91/131
            <Jonathan<John<John<the Frenchman
    Mary Ann McVicker-Cessna, bn 31 Jan 1783   91/131
        Wife of John
    Stephen Cessna, bn 1801   /131
    Jonathan Cessna, bn ca 1809   /131
    Nancy Cessna, bn 1802-08   /131
    Rebecca Cessna, bn 1802-08   /131
    Rachel Cessna, bn 1802-08   /131

7 Aug 1813, Estate of John Cessna, Colerain twp. Admin was Mary
Cessna & George James. Sureties by Jonathan Cessna.
3 Aug 1814, Ellis Rodgers of Bedford marries Rachel, d/o John Cessna,
dec'd of Colerain Twp.
1814 Cumberland Valley Twp Tax: John Cessna, 1 distillery, 2 horses,
4 cattle, farmer, $98 value: also, 45 A improved, 1 House,

Jno. Sisney   <William <John<the Frenchman

John Cessna, bn b4 1765		86/
wife, bn 1784-1765		86/
William Cessna, bn ca 1801		86/
Son, bn 1802		86/
Daughter, bn 1804		86/
Nancy Cessna, bn 1806		86/
Margaret Cessna, bn 1799		86/
Sara Cessna, bn 1797		86/

1820, William Cessna appeared in Census. He does not fit any other
family.
29 Feb 1824, Wm Boor married Sarah Cessna in Londonderry Twp,
Bedford County
20 July 1828, George Elder married Margarett Cessna in Londonderry
Twp. Bedford Co.
6 Sep 1829, James Elder married Nancy Cessna in Lodonderry Twp.
Bedford Co

Stephen Cisne bn 17-Apr-1782	91/135
<Jonathan<John<John<Frenchman	
Mary Rose-Cisne, bn 3 Mar 1787	/135
Married ca 1805	
Rebecca Cisne, bn 1809	/135
Emanuel Cisne, bn 4 Feb 1807	/135

Jonathan Sisney   <John<John<the Frenchman

Jonathan Cessna Sr, bn 16 Nov 1760	91/145
Rebecca Worley-Cessna, bn 16 Aug 1764	91/145
Joseph Cessna, bn 29 Oct 1801	91/135
William Cessna, bn 21 Dec 1797	91/145
Ezekiel Cessna, 12 May 1791	91/
Jonathan Cessna Jr, bn 1 April 1789	91/145
Eleanor Cessna, bn 16 Nov 1807	91/145
Rebecca Cessna, bn 5 Mar 1804	91/

Rachel Cessna, bn 1 June 1795   91/150
Sarah Cessna, bn 18 Nov 1786   91/142

3 June 1814, Jonathan Cessna purchased two shares of stock in Allegheny
      Bank of Pennsylvania
1815, Death of Rebecca Cessna, w/o Jonathan. Age 52, leaves 10
      children. Children John Cessna Sr: Stephen Cessna/Cisne,
      Charles Cessna, Sara are no longer in home. Sarah married Mr.
      Stephens
1814 Cumberland Valley Twp Tax: Jonathan Cessna, 320 A warranted,
      1 Distillery, $721 value. Also 50 a improved, $50 value.
      Tax for both is $6.62

Henry Williams   will die in 1815   90/
    Rebecca Cessna-Williams, 1 Aug 1762   90/146
        <John<John<Frenchman
    Hannah Williams, 24 May 1782   90/146
    John Williams, 30 Aug 1784   90/146
    Sarah "Sally" Williams, 1 Jul 1786   90/146
    Margaret P. Williams, 25 Feb 1789   90/146
    Elizabeth Williams, 12 Apr 1791   91/146
    Rebecca Williams, 4 Mar 1794   91/146
    Rachael Williams, 9 Apr 1797   91/146
    Mary Williams, 11 Mar 1800   91/146
    Eleanor "Nellie" Williams, 6 Oct 1802   91/146

Charles Cessna, bn 1762 <William<John<the Frenchman   91/142
    Rachel *Culbertson,* bn ca 1764   91/142
        (per daughter's gravestone) Married ca 1786
    William Franklin Cessna, bn ca 1786   91/142
    Rachel Cessna, born 1793   91/142
    Rebecca Cessna, ca 1790   87 /142
    Maria Cessna, ca 1795   87/142
    Mary Ann Cessna, (died unmarried)   87/

21 June 1794, Charles Cissna made a claim of 400 acres in Bedford
      County. Land is adjacent to that of Rachel Cessna. Family
      history reports he moved to Bedford County at that time.

William J. Vickory, bn 1768   92/146

    Elizabeth Cessna, bn 1768   92/146
        <John<John<The Frenchman

    Mary Cessna Vickory, bn 1796   92/146

    John Cessna Vickory, bn 1798   92/146

    William T. Vickory, bn 1800   92/146

    Joseph Vickory, bn 1802   /146

    Henry Vickory, bn 1804   /146

    Maria Vickory, bn 1810   /146

    James Ross Vickory, bn 2 Jan 1810   /146

Elizabeth Hall-Cessna   **w/o Maj John Cessna**

    Charles Hall Cessna   /148

    James Cessna   /149

    Sarah Rose Cessna

    Henry Cessna

1810 Napier twp

John Clark   bn ca 1776

    John Clark, Husband of Mary Cessna   121

    Mary Cessna-Clark, bn ca 1780   92/121
        <James<John<the Frenchman

    Son, bn 1800-1810   /121

    Daughter, bn 1800-1810   /121

William Cessna bn 20 Jun 1775   <John<John<the Frenchman

    William Cessna, Esq, 20 June 1775   90/147

    Nancy "Anna" Barnes-Cessna, bn 8 Feb 1779   90/144

    James H. Cessna, bn ca 1810   /144

    John Cessna, bn 3 Sep 1803   /144

    Eleanor Cessna, bn 6 Mar 1805*   /144

    Sarah Cissna, bn ca 1809   /144

    Ellen Cessna, bn 20 May 1807 *   /144

    Mary Cessna, bn 5 Aug 1801   /144

    Info from House of Cessna and Census

1810 Cumberland County
1810 Toboyne Twp

Stephen Cisna, bn 1766   <John<John<the Frenchman   93/152
   tephen Cessna/Cisna, bn 8 Dec 1766   93/152
   Mary Gardner-Cisna, bn ca 1768   93/152
   William Cisna, bn 1800   93/152
   John Cisna, bn ca 1791   93/152
   Lucinda Cisna, bn 1803   /152
   Mary Cisna, bn 1805   /152
   Eleanor Cisna, bn 1804   /152
   Rachel Cisna, bn ca 1795   93/152
   Julia Cisna, bn ca 1796   93/152
   Elizabeth Cisna, bn ca 1798   93/153

War of 1812 Enlistment records. John Sisney; 5'8: blue eyes, black hair,
    dark complexion, 34 or 35.
1811 Tax Toboyne Twp Cumberland County
    Stephen Sisna   50 ac land, $610: 96 acre Ridge land, $576
          1 horse & 3 cows $69,   total $1267
1814 Tax Toboyne Twp Cumberland County
    Stephen Cessna, 46 acres land
          3 acres land, 50 acres Ridge Land
          2 acres land, 46 acres Ridge Land $762
          One horse 2 cows

1810 Shippensburg

James Cessna, bn Apr 1751 <John<the Frenchman   92/149
   Mary ?-Cessna, bn Feb 1749   92/149
   John Cessna, bn ca 1780   92/149
   William Cessna, bn ca 1777   92/149
   Margaret Cessna, bn ca 1781 (never married)   92/149
   James Cessna Jr, bn ca 1784   92/139
   Mary Cessna, bn ca 1786   92/148
   Elizabeth Cessna, bn 10 Dec 1779   92/
   Sarah Cessna, bn ca 1788   92/

28 May 1814, John Cissna Pv US Light Dragoons; Cap John A. Bird; 5'
    10", blue eyes, brown hair, Dark complexion, 25, Farmer;

Shippensburg. Cumberland County, PA. Enlisted by Capt Burd for 5 yrs. Co Book 1812 to 1815. Present June 10 at Chambersburgh—Aug 9 at Carlisle—Nov 25/14 at Baltimore. 1812 to 1814 Harris Creek, Dec 31, 1814. Deserted from Baltimore, MD, Dec 4 or 5, 1814.

20 May 1812, John Cissna Pvt, 22nd US Infy; Col H. Brady; 5'9", blue eyes, dark hair, fair complexion, 34, farmer; Shippensburg, Cumberland County, PA. Enlisted at Shippensburg by Lieut Sturgess for 1 ½ years. Discharged Dec 20, 1813.

1833, In his will, James reports only 4 children still living.

1810 Fayette County
1810 Redstone Twp

Stephen Sisney bn ca 1767   95/150
         <Theophilus<Stephen<the Frenchman
    Stephen Cisna, bn ca 1766-1785   95/151
    Theophilus Cisna, bn ca 1785   95/151
         <Stephen<Theophilus<Stephen<the Frenchman
    Wife of Theophilus, bn 1775-85   95/151
       Son, bn 1806
       Daughter, bn 1808

1810 Franklin County
Fannettsburg Twp

Margaret Cisney, bn 1785 widow of   95/133
   Stephen<Theophilus<Stephen<the Frenchman
    Theophilus, bn 1805-1810   95/
    Daughter, bn 1805-1810

1808, Father-in-law, William Cisna moved to Greenville, SC. Son is probably named James.

Thomas Cissna, bn 1760   <Theophilus<Stephen<the Frenchman   94/151
    Mrs. ?-Cisna, bn ca 1760   94/151
    Thomas Henderson Cisna, bn 1778   94/151
    Archibald Cisna, bn ca 1782   94/151
    John Alfred Cisna, bn ca 1785   94/151
    William Henry Cisna, bn ca 1787   94/151
    David Alexander Cisna, bn ca 1789   94/151

    16 May 1813, Thomas Cissna, pri, US Arty, Late Capt Grano, 5'6 ½",
        hazel eyes, sandy hair, ruddy complection, 35 yrs, Tailor from
        Shippensburgh, PA. Enlisted, by Capt Humphres. Discharged at
        New Orleans Apr 9, 1815. This would be Thomas Henderson
        Cisna.

Theophilus Cisney, bn 1760   <John<the Frenchman   95/152
    Betsey Cisney, bn ca 1797   95/152
    Martha "Agnes" Cisney, bn ca 1796   95/152
    Stephen Cisney, bn ca 1799   95/152
    James Cisney, bn ca 1794   95/152
    Nancy Richardson-Cisney, bn ca 1770   95/152
    William Cisney, bn 1802   /152
    Thomas Cisney, bn 14 June 1808   /152

    Info from House of Cessna.

James Cisna, bn ca 1782   96/148
        <Theophilus<Stephen<the Frenchman
    Wife of James, bn ca 1781   96/148
    Washington Cisna, bn ca 1798   96/148
    Thomas Cisna, bn ca 1800   96/148

    Names provided by House of Cessna but not dates.
    James Cisney, company of Capt William Strain, of 6th battalion 1780.
        This unit from Lurgan Twp.
    1781, James Cesna, fifer for Capt William Strain's company, 22 days in.
        William Cesna was pvt.

1810 Huntington County

Theophilus J. Cisna, bn c 1782   96/150
        <Thomas<Theophilus<Stephen<the Frenchman
        Margaret McGuire-Cisna, bn ca 1782   96/150

1810 South Carolina

1810 Greenville District

William Sisney, bn ca 1764   <Theophilus<Stephen<the Frenchman   91/
        Wife of William Cis*na,* bn ca 1770
        George Cissna bn ca1800
        Daughter, bn ca 1793

      1810 Census of Greenville District, South Carolina   no twp listed
           William Sisney
     No evidence to corroborate that this is part of the family. But his
          birthdate aligns with son of Theophilus bn in Franklin County
     Unable to find him in future census.

Mississippi in 1804

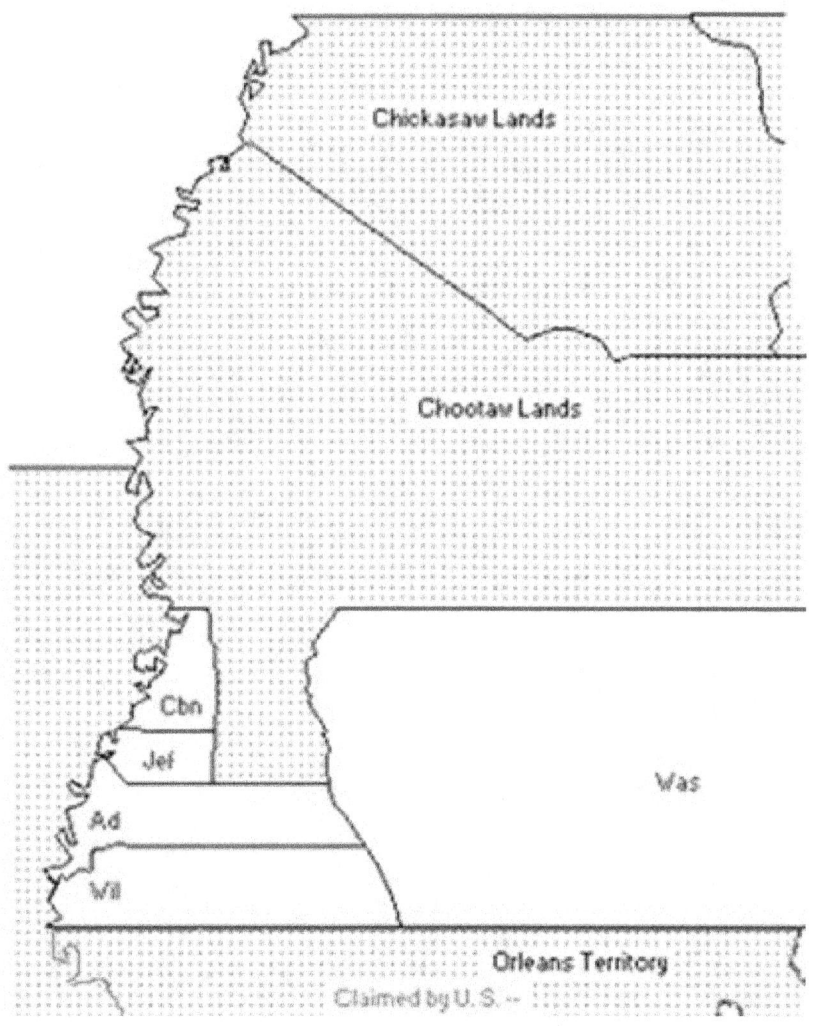

1820 CENSUS

1820 Georgia

1820 Morgan County

Robert Baker Cessna, bn 1786   97/
<Samuel<Charles<John<the Frenchman
No family. 7 slaves

1815, Robert Cessna paid tax in Greene County
1817, Robert Cessna paid tax in Morgan County
Note: He did not move. County lines changed.

Robert Cessna, bn 1803   93/
<Robert<Samuel<Charles<John<the Frenchman
No family. 4 slaves

Samuel Cessna, bn ca 1790   93/
<Samuel<Charles<John<the Frenchman
Elizabeth Huddleston-Cessna

20 Sept 1820, Samuel married Elizabeth Huddleston

Elizabeth Cessna, bn 1787   93/
<Samuel<Charles<John<the Frenchman
Have found no record of her marriage

1820 Indiana

1820 Spencer County
Rockport

Stephen P. Cissna, bn 1785   <Joseph<John<the Frenchman   101/
Margaret McFarling-Cissna, bn ca 1800   101/
Amanda Jane Cissna, bn 1810   101/

/

1819, Amanda's mother, Mary Moore, (Stephen's 1st wife) died.

20 Nov 1820, Stephen P. Cissna married Margaret McFarling

Stephen was the first physician in Rockport, IN. He studied medicine as a
surgeon's assistant during the War of 1812. Finished his
apprentice, and moved from Chillicothe, OH to
Spencer County, IN about 1818.

Dr. Stephen P. Cissna was said to have discovered an almost infallible
cure for Milk Sickness.

25 Oct 1829, Amanda Jane Cissna married John Pitcher

Joseph Cissna, bn 24 June 1789   <Joseph<John<the Frenchman   101/

23 Mar 1823, Joseph Cissna married Susannah Young in Spencer County,
IN.

10 June 1818, Joseph bought a town lot in Rockport. This was a large
auction selling many town lots. The price range was $5 to $500.

1818 Joseph Cissna came to Rockport with his brother, Stephen P. Cissna
from Chillicothe, OH. Joseph was a saddler and Stephen the first
Physician in town.

David M. Cissna   101/
Reputed to be a brother of Stephen P and Joseph Cissna.

Nov 1832 David Cissna voted in the Presidential Election while in
Spencer County, IN.

1 Nov 1833 David M. Cissna is a witness in estate of Jacob Brant.

15 Apr 1835 Susannah Allensworth is granted a continuance in her suit
against David M. Cissna and others, over debts owed to her.

1838 David Cissna is Marshal for Spencer County, IN

UNKNOWN IN INDIANA:
1820 Indiana

Could find no evidence in the census, but the following
information indicates that these persons were alive and possibly
living in Indiana in 1820.

Decatur County, IN
17 Sep 1823, **Jason Cisne** married Betty Jane Tremain

Wabash County, IN
1820 Census (p 221), William Siseney: 1 male under 10,
1 male 26-44; 2 females under 10; 2 females 16-25

1820 Kentucky

1820 Christian County
Along the Pond River

Robert Sessney, bn ca 1788   98/
    Robert Cisney, bn ca 1789   98/
      <Stephen<John<Stephen<the Frenchman
    Mary Gatting-Cisney, bn ca 1790
    Andrew Posey Cisney, bn ca 1819
    George Washington Cisney, bn 1810   98/
    Robert A. Cisney, bn 36 June 1814
    Franklin "Frank" Cisney,   98/
      (nephew)   *<unknown<Stephen<the Frenchman*
    Male, under 10, bn ca 1817

1810 Census Christian County   p 14 or 533
    Robert Sisney 0/0/1/0/0/1/0/1/
1814-1815, Robert Cisney volunteered to serve in War of 1812
1826, another daughter was born but did not survive.
5 Jan 1824, Estate of Robert Cisney, listed goods.

Stephen Sessney   <John<Stephen<the Frenchman
    Stephen Sisney, bn 1745   98/
    Dolly Holten-Sisney, bn ca 1760   98/

1810 Census Christian County   p 14 or 533
    Stephen Sisney   0/1/0/0/1/0/0/0/0/1
9 Sept 1823, Will of Stephen Sisney: land, house stock and property to
    provide for wife Dolly. After her death it shall go to grandson
    George Washington Sisney, son of Robert and Mary his wife.
    Daughters: Mary Grace and Rachel Taylor and Elizabeth Ray,
    five shillings each.

Stephen William Sisney, bn ca 1795   98/
    Betsy Troyver-Sisney, bn ca 1800
    David S. Sisney, bn 1820

15 July 1816, Stephen Sisney married Betsy Troyver in Christian County.
    Stephen Sisney and Mrs. Brown secure bonds for the marriage.

1817. Stephen Cisney sold half to Stephen Cisney Jr. Deed Book P page
45 "Being in Christian County on waters of Pond River; being
the Northwest corner of a Survey of land granted to said Cisney
Senior on 31st Day of October 1817, of 175 acres.
Stephen Cisney Sr sold to Robert Cisney. Deed Book P, page
214. "part of a tract of land containing 175 acres bounded as
follows; beginning at a white oak corner of Stephen Cisneys
land......'till it strikes a hickory, corner of Stephen Cissney Jr's,
survey."

1820 Hardin County
Little York

Wm Cisna <Jonathan<John<the Frenchman		98/
William Cessna, bn 17 June 1776		98/
"Sally" Wallace-Cessna, bn 1778		98/
Jonathan Friend Cessna, bn 16 Nov 1804		98/
Margaret Cessna, bn ca 1819		
Susan Cessna, bn 1817		
Matilda Cessna, bn ca 1815		
Nancy Cessna, bn ca 1812		
Mary Cessna, bn ca 1807		98/
Elizabeth "Betsey" Cessna, bn ca 1808		98/
William Wallace Cessna, born 2 May 1822		

12 April 1802, William W. Cessna married Sarah Wallace in Hardin
County.

Sheperd Gum

Nancy Agnes Cessna-Gum, bn ca 1774	99/
<Jonathan<John<the Frenchman	

1820 Kenton County, KY

Solomon Rees
Mary Cissna-Rees 106/
Possibly<Thomas<Evans<John<Frenchman

1820, Names of daughters taken from Estate Papers: June 1820: Margaret Cissna; Flora Cissna; heirs of Thomas Cissna vs. Morris Rees; Thomas Rees; Jesse Rees; Larkin Reynolds and Sarah, his wife, formerly Sarah Rees, daughter of said Thomas; Mary Rees and Solomon Rees, heirs at law of said Thomas: also Noah Zane, John Smith and Mathew Ewing. Said Thomas Rees, Larkin Reynolds and wife Sarah; Mary Rees, Solomon Rees and Noah Zane are not residents of this state.

1820 Muhlenberg County

Elizabeth Culbertson-Cessna, bn ca 1780 wife of 99/
Robert<Charles<John<the Frenchman
Sarah "Sally" Culbertson Cessna, bn 1808 99/
Elizabeth Cessna, bn 1795 99/
Mary E. Cessna, bn ca 1798 99/
Nancy Cessna, bn 16 Mar 1801 99/
Johanna L. Cessna, bn 2 Feb 1803 99/
Margaret "Peggy" D. Cessna, bn ca 1805 99/
Charles Cessna, bn ca 1806 99/
Robert John Culberson Cessna, born 7 Apr 1814
3 slaves

11 July 1814, Elizabeth Cessna, widow of Robert Cessna was granted Administrators: Robert Glen, James Milligan & James Sharp. Heirs are Mary Cessna, Nancy Cessna, Joanna Cessna, Sally Cessna, Charles Cessna, Margaret Cessna and Robert J. Cessna.

James Milligan 96/
Following children: <Elizabeth<Charles<John<the Frenchman
Melia Milligan, bn 1794 96/
Melinda Milligan, I Jul 1795 96/
Charles Milligan, 20 Jan 1800 96/
James Milligan, bn 1802 96/
William M. C. Milligan, bn 21 Jan 1807 96/

Roseanna Milligan, 12 Feb 1809   96/
Johanna Milligan, bn 7 Jun 1811
Joseph Milligan, bn 25 Mar 1814
Esther "Hettie" Milligan, bn 1 Jun 1816

1817-1819, Elizabeth Cessna-Milligan died

John C. Millegan, 20 December 1789   95/
                <Elizabeth<Charles<John<the Frenchman
Elizabeth Cessna-Millegan, bn 1795   95/
                <Robert<Charles<John<the Frenchman
Son of John & Elizabeth, bn ca 1818
Son of John & Elizabeth, bn ca 1819

5 April 1817, Elizabeth married John, they had 5 boys & 2 girls,
    according to family tradition.

James Sharp   100/
Sarah "Sally" Sharp, bn 1780   100/
                <William<William<John<Frenchman
Robert Cessna Sharp, bn 7 Oct 1804   100/
Samuel Cessna Sharp, bn 26 Jan 1803   100/
William McCormic Sharp, bn 22 Feb 1806   100/
Charles Culbertson Sharp, bn 22 Ap 1808   100/
John Nelson Sharp, bn1811
Son, bn ca 1813

1820, Sally Cessna-Sharp died in Central City, Muhlenberg County

1820 Michigan

1820 Wayne County

Hiram Jones
    Jeanne Cissne-Jones,   107/
              <William<Joseph<John<the Frenchman
    Son under age 10

John Macomb
    Sarah Cissna-Corbus-Macomb, bn 1782   100/
              <Joseph<John<the Frenchman
    Richard W. Corbus, bn ca 1801   100/
    Joseph Cissna Corbus, bn ca 1803   100/
    John Corbus, bn ca 1805   100/
    James G. Corbus, bn ca 1806   100/

1807, Godfrey Corbus died. She later married John Macomb.

1820 Missouri

Robert Cisna, bn ca 1785-92   106/
    <Evans<John<the Frenchman

May 1817, Stephen Glasscock made a survey of Township N 56, of
        baseline, in Range #19 west of 5th Principal Meridian, showing
        Robert Cisna owns 40 acres, #7776.

1820 Mississippi

1820 Adams County
Natchez

William W. Cisna Jr., bn ca 1781   104/
    <William W.<William<John<the Frenchman
    Wife ?-Cessna, bn ca 1785

Son of William, bn 1816-20
Daughter of William, bn 1816-20

Another son and two daughters will be born in the 1820's
1816 Census of Jefferson County, MS
        William Cissna Jr, 2/0/1/3/0/3
        2 WM over 21; 1 WF over 21; 3 WF under 21; 3 slaves
        William Cissna Sr, 7/0/0/0/7/3/7
        7 WM over 21; no females; 3 free persons of color; 7 slaves
1820 Census of Adams County, MS
        William Cesna, 3 males 16-26, 4 females 16-26

William W. Cessna bn 1768 1/3/1/0/0/5   103/
    William Cessna Sr, bn 1768
        <William<John<the Frenchman
    Margaret *Robinette*-Cessna, bn ca 1770   103/
    John Cessna, bn 1793   103/
    James Cessna, bn 1798   103/
    John Robinette, bn ca 1790   103/

1820 Census of Adams County, MS
        William Cisson, 1 males 10-15; 2 males 26-44; 1 female over
        45; 1 female slave 26-44, two persons in agriculture.

S.W.H. Cissna, bn ca 1800 unknown<unknown<the Frenchman

23 Aug 1821, S.W.H. Cessna married H Maria Fuller in Natchez. When
        they maried, Maria had a daughter under age 5.
Sept 1823, S.W.H. Cissna, editor of Natchez paper, has died of the
        pestilence at Natchez.
1830, Maria Cissna was a resident in Natchez

1820 Jefferson County

Charles Cessna, bn 1795 <*unknown*<Charles<John<the Frenchman
    Charles Cissna, bn ca 1795   102/
    Catherine Brady-Cissna, bn 1795
    John Cessna, bn 1820
    Male, over 45 Mr. Brady (f-in-law) bn b4 1775
    Mary Cessna, bn 1820
    Female, over 45 Mrs. Brady (m-in-law), bn b4 1775
    2 Slaves

27 Nov 1819, Charles Cessna married Catherine Brady
29 May 1848, John Cessna married Rebecca Waller
14 May 1857, Mary Cessna married John Robinett

Joseph Cessna, bn ca 1785   102/
  < *unknown* <Charles<John<the Frenchman

Culbertson D. Cessna, bn 19 Feb 1789   102/
  < *unknown* <Charles<John<the Frenchman

  Ca 1821, Culbertson left the Cessna family farm and move to
    Yazoo, County to be with Robinette family.
  22 Feb 1822, Culbertson Cissna married Margarette Robinnette

1820 Claiborne County

Aaron Neel
  Aaron Neel, (husband of Mary Cessna)   102/
   all these children…<Mary<Charles<John<the Frenchman
  Robert Neel, bn 1805-1810   103/
  Thomas S. Neel, bn 1802-1804   103/
  Carolyn Neel, bn 1800-1810   103/
  Lurenna Smith Neel, bn 1800-1810   103/

1820, Mary Cessna-Neel appears to be deceased
8 Oct 1821, Estate of Aaron Neel. John C. Neel and Charles Neel are
  appointed executors posting $600 bond with William Cessna and
  Francis Tidwell as securities.
July 1822, Orphans court: John C and Charles Neel post appraisal of
  Aaron Neel's property.

Charles Cessna Neel, bn ca 1795   103/
  <Mary<Charles<John<the Frencnman
  Emeline ?-Neel, bn ca 1800

William S. Cessna bn Jul 1791<unknown<Charles<John<Frenchman   102/

  Appears to still be living with Aaron Neel family.
  21 Aug 1823, Wm. Cessna married Elizabeth Young in Jefferson County.

1820 North Carolina

1820 Buncombe County

Green Kennedy Cessna bn 1805   105/
                <John<John<Charles<John<the Frenchman
      Male 10-20 **Brother of Green K Cessna**
      Male 10-20 **Brother of Green K Cessna**
      Male 10-20 **Brother of Green K Cessna**
      Male 10-20 **William D. Cessna**   Brother of Green K Cessna   105/
      male 20-30 **Brother of Green K Cessna**
      female 5-10 **Sister of Green K Cessna**
      female 5-10 **Sister of Green K Cessna**
      Female 5-10 **Sister of Green K Cessna**
      Female 5-10 **Sister of Green K Cessna**
      Female 10-20 **Sister of Green K Cessna**
      one person over 15 deaf and dumb.

    It appears that Green Kennedy has inherited the leadership of his
           father's household between 1810 and 1820. The home has
           no matriarch. And the numbers of children indicate that some
           may be his nieces and nephews.
    Green Kennedy Cessna did not marry until 1829.
    July 1820 Elizabeth Cessna and two sons: Green and William D. applied
           for land warrants in Jackson County, TN. Near Buncombe
           County, NC.

John Cessna, bn ca 1764 <Charles<John<the Frenchman
    John Cessna, bn 1760   104/
    Wife of John, bn ca 1765   103/
    G- Son, bn 1810-1820
    G-Son, bn 1810-1820
    G -Daughter, bn 1810-1820
    10 Slaves

    This is the grandfather of Green Kennedy Cessna below. He seems to be
           caring for his daughter and her children.
    1830 Census Buncombe County, NC. This John appears again:
           John Cessna 60-69 (1760-1770) 1 male 10-14; 1 male 15-19;
           1 female 10-14; 1 Female 15-19; 1 female 60-69 (1760-1770).
    20 Aug 1832, Henry Brooksire sold to Richard Cisna 50 acres on
           Hawkins Mill Creek.
    Note: This family is much smaller than it was in 1810. Why?

1820 Ohio

1820 Coshocton County
1820 Perry Twp

Charles Cissna   <Jonathan<John<John<the Frenchman
    Charles Cessna, bn 4 Feb 1784   106/
    Ann?-Cessna, wife of Charles   106/
    Jonathan Cessna, bn 1818
    James O. Cessna, bn 1809   106/
    Rebecca Cessna, bn 1810-1820
    Mary C. Cessna. bn 21 Jun 1820
    Sarah Cessna, bn 17 Jan 1813
    Nancy Cisney, bn ca 1810   106/

1814, Charles Cessna and Nathan Wright came to Coshocton County
         from Perry Township in Bedford County, PA
Between 1820 and 1830, Charles was be joined in Perry Twp of
         Coshocton County by his brothers John and Jonathan.
1823, A Christian Church vulgarly known as "New Light" was organized
         with Charles Cessna and his family as members.
1824, School started in Coshocton County by Wm McCoy. Three Cessna
         families sent their children there.
27 Nov 1828, Nancy Cisney married William Lemert in Coshocton Cty.
20 Dec 1832, Jonathan Cessna married Margaret Diven in Coshocton Cty
3 June 1830, James Cessna married Mary Parker in Coshocton County

John Cessna, bn 26 Aug 1780   112/
                 <Jonathan<John<John<the Frenchman
    Mary Ann McVicker-Cessna, bn 31 Jan 1783   112/
      Wife of John
    Stephen Cessna, bn 1801   112/
    Jonathan Cessna, bn ca 1809   112/
    Nancy Cessna, bn 1802-08   112/
    Rebecca Cessna, bn 1802-08   112/
    Rachel Cessna, bn 1802-08   112/

1822, John Cessna moved to Coshocton County, OH
1825, John Cessna paid tax in Coshocton County.

22 Apr 1832, John Cessna died in Coshocton County.
Note: Family entered on page 142

1820 Fairfield County

Margaret Cissna, bn b4 1775 (Widow of Thomas)   106/
    Flora Cissna, bn 1810-1820   106/
        <Thomas<Evans<Charles<the Frenchman
    Eliza Cissna, bn 1804-1810   106/
        <Thomas<Evans<Charles<the Frenchman
    Maria Cissna, bn 1804-1810   106/
        <Thomas<Evans<Charles<the Frenchman
    Hannah Cissna/Rees/Paxton, bn 1801-1804   106/
        <Thomas<Evans<Charles<the Frenchman
    Robert Cissna, bn 1800   (bro-in-law)   106/
        <Thomas<Evans<Charles<the Frenchman

1802, Thomas Cissna married Margaret sometimes called "Peggy"
1817, Estate of Thomas Cissna of Fairfield Co. Margaret is his wife. He
    died on a trading expedition to New Orleans.
8 Jan 1821, Margaret "Peggy" Cissna, w/o Thomas died in Fairfield
    County.
1822, Robert Cisne furnished $5 in work to help build the Presby church
    in Fairfield County.
1825, Robert Cissna married Susan McCullom
Larkin Reynolds may have moved to Abbeville, South Carolina, as hinted
    by Census records in 1850.
Solomon Rees seems to have moved to Kenton County, KY.

1820 Holmes County

Evans Cisney,   111/
    < Charles Sisney<Jonathan<John<John<the Frenchman

1825, Evans Cisney paid tax in Holmes County.

1820 Guernsey County
1820 Bea Twp

John Cissney, bn 1790-1800
>> unknown<John<the Frenchman
> **Wife of John,** bn ca 1797
> **Agnes Cisney,** bn ca 1819
> **Ellen Cisney,** bn ca 1818
> **Stephen Cisney,** bn ca 1812

> 10 Dec 1840, Agnes Cisney married William Ankron
> 12 Jan 1839, Ellen Cisney married Robert Wait
> 28 April 1836, Stephen Cisney married Elizabeth Gibbons at Senecaville

1820 Lawrence County

1820 Decatur Twp

Margaret Sisney,   female 26-45 bn 1775-1794   117/
> Widow of James <William<Theophilus<Stephen<the Frenchman

> It appears that her daughter and son-in-law, Joseph Lewis
>> Thompson, are living next door to her at this time.

1820 Madison County
1820 London Twp

James Cisna,   <Samuel<Evans<Charles**James Cessna,** bn ca 1796
> **Elizabeth Ann Bird-Cessna,** bn ca 1801
> 1 male over 45? Father in law?

> James and partner opened a saddle shop in the new town of London.

1820 Range Twp

Samuel Cissna, bn ca 1781   <Evans<John<the Frenchman   104/
    Samuel Cissna, bn ca 1781   104/
    Mary Wilcutt-Cissna, bn ca 1783   104/
    David Cisna, bn 1806   104/
    John Cissna, bn 1807   104/
    Charles Cissna, bn 1808   104/
    Robert Cissna, bn 1809   104/
    Maryette Cissna, bn 1816
    Unknown boy, bn ca 1815
    Unknown girl, bn ca 1819

1800, Samuel was a tailor in Pittsburgh during the flood
1810, Samuel paid. tax to Ross Co., OH
1820 Madison County Census - Union Twp.
Note: When the State Capitol was moved from Chillicothe to Columbus,
    Samuel moved his family to Madison County.

William Cissna, 1781   <Stephen<Thomas<Stephen<Frenchman   104/
    William Cissna, bn 1781-90
    Margaret Hall-Cissna, bn ca 1790
    Son, bn 1810-1820
    Daughter, bn 1810-1820
    Female, over 45   Margaret Hagen-Cissna?   104/

War of 1812 Bounty Lands in IL says: 31 Dec 1817 #13817 Wm. Cisna,
    musician in Bell's 28th Inf. - Land: NW23, 14N, Twp. 8 E.
    Range. Delivered to Wm. Cissna of Chillicothe, OH. He
    later sold this land never having been there to see it.
19 Mar 1815, Married Margaret Hall in Madison County.
1830 Census: William is in Jackson Twp age 40-50

1820 Monroe County

Jonathan Cisne <unknown

1825, Jonathan Cisne paid tax in Monroe County

Possibly; Jonathan<Jonathan<John<John<Frenchman who moved from Bedford to Coshocton County, Oh in 1826

Stephen Cisne, bn 17-Apr-1782   113/
        <Jonathan<John<John<Frenchman
Mary Rose-Cisne, bn 3 Mar 1787   113/
        Married ca 1805
Rebecca Cisne, bn 1809   113/
Stephen Sylvester Cisne, bn 11 Nov 1811
Emanuel Cisne, bn 4 Feb 1807   113/
Jonathan Cisne, bn 19 May 1815
Eleanor Cisne, bn 27 May 1817
Sarah Cisne, bn 16 Jan 1819
Agnes Cisne, bn 13 Sept 1821
May Cisne,
Ezekiel Cisne, bn 17 Apr 1826
Margaret Ann Cisne, bn 20 Sep 1829

1815, Stephen moved to Monroe County on Sunfish Creek
1821, Stephen Cisney paid tax in Monroe County.
1825, Stephen Cisney paid tax in Monroe County

1820 Pike County
1820 Piketon

Charles Cissna,   <Stephen<Thomas<Stephen<the Frenchman
      Charles Cissna, bn 19 Sep 1815   109/
      Dorcus Wilcut-Cissna, bn ca 1788   109/
      John B. Cissna, bn 7 Nov 1810   109/
      David Cissna, bn 4 Oct 1808   109/
      Evans Cissna, bn ca 1802   109/
      Unknown male, bn 16-25
      James Cissna, bn ca 1789   109/
            <Stephen<Thomas<Stephen<the Frenchman
      George Cissna, bn ca 1795   109/
            <Stephen<Thomas<Stephen<the Frenchman
      Unknown male, bn 1795-1804   109/

Charles Cissna, bn 2 Feb 1783   109/
Julia Ann Cissna, 10 bn ca 1817
Elizabeth Ann Cissna 10 bn ca 1819
Mary, H. B. Cissna, bn 1 July 1806   109/

Note: When the State Capitol was moved from Chillicothe to Columbus,
      Charles and Dorcus relocated to Piketon. His father and mother
      being elderly, Charles's younger half-brother moved with them.
1819, Charles Cissna vs Abraham Shane over a debt due.

Joseph Cissna   <Stephen<Thomas<Stephen<the Frenchman
    Joseph Cissna, bn ca 1790   104/
    Wife of Joseph, bn ca 1795
    Son, bn 1810-1820

1820 & 1826, Joseph granted tavern lic. for house in Piketon, OH.

1820 Ross County

Joseph Cissna, bn 1774   <Joseph<Unknown<the Frenchman   109/
    Wife of Joseph Cissna, (Ms Howe?)   109/
    Joseph P. Cissna, bn 1801   109/
    Malinda Cissna, bn ca 1795   109/
    Mary Cissna, bn ca 1799, d 14 Sept 1780

1809 Scioto Twp tax: Joseph Ceeney, 140 A square, adjoining Chillicothe
    on the Scioto River.
1809 Union Twp Tax: Joseph Cissna, 113 A, originally owned by
    Nathaniel Massie on Scioto River.
20 June 1815, Melinda Cissna to Robert Chelfin (Malinda d/o of Stephen
    would only be 16 yrs old.)
1821, Joseph P. Cissna married Asenith Repose in Ross County.
    They named their son Robert Howe Cissna.
20 Mar 1821, Mary Cissna married Eleazer P. Beard in Chillicothe

Stephen Cissna   <Thomas<Stephen<the Frenchman   108/
   Stephen Cissna, bn 1755   108/
   Margaret Hegan-Cissna, bn ca 1770   108/
      Wife of Stephen Cissna Sr.
   Baldwin Cissna, bn 28 Oct 1807, d 30 Aug 1823   108/
   Elizabeth Cissna, bn 1799   108/
   Stephen Cissna Jr, bn ca 1795   108/
      <Stephen<Thomas<Stephen<the Frenchman
   Sarah Finnimore King-Cissna, bn 1775-1794
      Wife of Stephen Cissna Jr.
      William Cissna, bn 17 June 1816
      <Stephen<Stephen<Thomas<Stephen<the Frenchman
      Stephen A. Cissna, 9 Feb 1815
      <Stephen<Stephen<Thomas<Stephen<the Frenchman
    Daughter, of Stephen Jr. bn 1810-1820
    Daughter, of Stephen Jr. bn 1804-1810   108/

Enlisted at Bedford, PA in 1775 as Pvt. Sharpshooter, marched to
    Boston, Stationed at Lechmere's Point, under Capt. Robert
    Cluggage's Co., Col.Thompson's Reg. Rec'd pension #S42647
    issued Nov. 1818 for $8.00 mo. After 1 yr. of service, he vol. &
    served in various calls until end of war. S.A.R. marker on grave.
    1st bur. in Presby. Cem. but moved by Scioto Valley R.R. in
    1869 to Greenlawn along w/sons Baldwin & John & John's son
    Samuel. Was on various jurys in Pittsburgh, PA, Sep. 1789-
    Dec. 1792 and Grand Jury 1790 & 1791.
1801-1820, Stephen's wife was referred to as "Polly" in most of the
    deeds. In one she was called "Mary" in another, "Margaret".
4 Feb 1822, Malinda Cissna married Samuel Porter in Chillicothe 14 Aug
1823, Stephen Cissna Sr. died in Chillicothe. Baldwin seems to
    have been born with disabilities and died 30 Aug 1823.
27 Sep 1823, Margaret rec'd his final pension for $89.54.
28 May 1821, Stephen Cissna bought Chillicothe lot 30 from
    William Clark for $200
3 Sep 1823, Stephen Cissna bought Chillicothe lot 27 from
    Richard Fleming for $60
3 Aug 1824, Samuel Cissna sold Chillicothe lot 223 (E half) to
    Thomas B. Armsrong for $26
26 Feb 1814, Stephen Cissna, bn 1794 in Pittsburgh, married Sarah King
    in Chillicothe. Stephen fought under Capt Brush in War, was
    given an invalid pension. Stephen will die of his wounds in
    1830. His children Stephen and William found Cissna Park, IL
6 Oct 1817, Stephen Cisna, private in Gills 19th Infantry, receives patent
    for land; NW 8 ¼ * 11 S twp* 2 W Range.

Samuel Porter
> **Eleanor Cissna,** bn ca 1800　　　　　　　　　　　108/
> <Stephen<Thomas<Stephen<The Frenchman

> 4 Feb 1820,　Eleanor married Samuel Porter in Chillicothe.

James Cissna, bn ca 1789　　　　　　　　　　　　108/
> <Stephen<Thomas<Stephen<The Frenchman
> **Catherine Ewing**

> 20 May 1818, James Cissna married Catherine Ewing

John Renshaw
> **Malinda Cissna/Chelfin/Renshaw,** bn ca 1798　　108/
> <Stephen<Thomas<Stephen<The Frenchman
> **Chelfin Daughter,** bn ca 1817

> 20 June 1815, Malinda Cissna married Robert Chelfin.
> 7 Sep 1820, Malinda Cissna re-married to John Renshaw in Ross County.
> They will have two daughters in the next decade.

John Cissna, bn 1779　　　　　　　　　　　　　108/
> <Stephen<Thomas<Stephen<the Frenchman
> **Elizabeth Moore-Cissna,** bn ca 1779　　　　　108/
> **Robert Cissna,** bn 30Apr 1800　　　　　　　　108/
> **Elizabeth Cissna,** bn ca 1802　　　　　　　　108/
> **Jane Cissna,** bn 1804　　　　　　　　　　　　108/
> **Charles Cissna,** bn 4 Dec 1808　　　　　　　　108/
> **William M. Cissna,** bn ca 1810　　　　　　　　108/
> **Samuel Cissna,** bn Sep 1814,　d 4 Mar 1718
> **Rose Ann Cissna,** bn ca 1816
> **James Cissna,** bn 17 June 1818

> Nov 1819, John bought land in Huntington Twp., Ross Co., OH
> 3 Sept 1821, John Cissna died of illness contracted during War of 1812
> 9 Nov 1821, John Cissna was deceased. Elizabeth & Robert Cessna are
> administrators.
> 30 June 1824, Elizabeth Cessna married Thomas Wilson in Ross County
> 12 Dec 1821, Sarah Cissna married Noah Justice in Ross County
> 4 Feb 1822, Eleanor Cissna married Samuel Porter in Ross County

Evans Cissna, bn ca 1797 <unknown<the Frenchman
    Margaret McCrary-Cissna, bn ca 1797

19 May 1817, Evans Cissna married Margaret McCrary in Ross County

1820 Scioto County
1820 Decatur Twp

James Cissna bn 1791   <James<John<the Frenchman
    James Cissna, bn 1778   ca 1790   116/
    Wife of James, bn ca 1789
    Son, bn 1810-1820
    Son, bn 1810-1820
    Son, bn 1810-1820
    Daughter, bn 1810-1820

James was executor of his father's estate in Cumberland County 1833.

1820 Wayne County
1820 Prairie Twp

James Cissney, bn ca 1776 <Joseph<John<the Frenchman
    James Cissne   107/
    Elizabeth Cessna-Cissne, bn ca 1780   107/
            <James<John<the Frenchman
    William Cissna Jr., bn 1806   107/
    John Cissna * **, bn 1802   107/
    Ann Cissna, bn 1810*   107/
    Margaret Cissne, bn 1816
    Sarah Cissna*, bn 1811   107/
    Jane Cissne, bn 1803   107
    Joseph Cissne, bn ca 1821

*1814, James became the legal guardian of his brother William's (>Capt
Joseph Cissna>John Cessna>Jean de Cesne), orphaned children:
Anne (1799 MI), John (1800 MI), Jane (1803 MI), Sarah (1804
MI), William Jr. (1806 MI).
1823, James Cissne, "land on Hamtrack. This claim originally
numbered by the Commissioners of Claims"
1810, James Cissna was one of the 1st settlers in Franklin Twp., Wayne
Co., OH. Purchased. land in Prairie Twp. Moved to Ohio from
Michigan.
22 May 1813, James purchased lot 10 in Wooster, OH, Wayne County.
James stayed in Holmes County until his death 12 May 1839. Elizabeth
died 12 Apr 1839).
**John Cissna married Hannah Charlton on 10 June 1824.

George W. Armstrong Sr.

Anne Cissna-Armstrong, bn 8 March 1799   107/
<William<Joseph<John<Jean de Cesna
Jane Armstrong, bn 1820

11 Feb 1819, Anne Cissna married George Armstrong in Wayne Co, OH

John Cissney, bn 1775   <Joseph<John<the Frenchman   107/
Jane Glass-Cissna, bn 1778   107/
John Cissna Jr, bn 1814
Robert Cissna, bn 23 Oct 1811
Joseph Glass Cissna, bn 25 Feb 1809   107/
John Cissna, bn 1775   107/
Mary "Polly" Cissna, bn 29 Nov 1817
Elizabeth Cissna, bn 13 Sep 1806   107/
Sara Cissna, bn 1821

About 1806, James and John Cissna (sons of Capt Joseph Cissna) travel
up Killbuck Creek in a dugout canoe to trade with the Wyandot
Indian villages. As soon as these lands became available to
purchase, they did so. John and Joseph helped keep the
Wyandot Indians loyal to the US during the War of 1812.
1812, John was made Probate Judge when Holmes county organizes.
In early 1830, John moved his family to LaPorte County, IN.
1803, John was an Ensign in Detroit Militia in.

Jonathan Alexander de Cessna, bn 1802 (aka John Cessna)
<James<John<the Frenchman
Susan Beechler-Cessna

Jonathan married Susan Beechler about 1829. Family reports he was born in Michigan in 1802, In 1830 Census of Holmes County, they have no children.

The children of John Beechler Cessna report the following: Jonathan Alexander Pinkerton De Cessna was a Rev War hero. He fathered Jonathan Alexander Cissna in Michigan about 1802. He fathered John Beechler Cissna who was born in 1831 in Holmes County. No records of these three individuals have been found in Census, land or legal records. So this branch of the family dead ends at John Beechler Cissna.

HOWEVER: The House of Cessna reports that two children of James, < John<the Frenchman; moved to Holmes County, OH to be with the children of his brother, Capt. Joseph Cissna of Detroit. Elizabeth Cessna (youngest child of James) married her cousin James Cissna (son of Capt. Joseph) and raised a family in Wayne/Holmes County, Ohio following the War of 1812. Elizabeth's brother John came to join them about 1818 and raised a family in Holmes County. The House of Cessna reports that John Cessna fathered four sons and two daughters between 1820 and 1835 in Holmes County. But House of Cessna did not provide names for these children. This seems to be the most obvious lineage for John Beechler Cessna, born 1831 in Holmes County.

1820 Pennsylvania

1820 Allegheny County
1820 St. Clair Twp

Theophilus Cisney,   112/
    Theophilus Cisney, bn 1720-30   <Stephen<the Frenchman
    Unknown Male, bn 1805-10 (probably a grandson)
        <unknown<Theophilus<Stephen<the Frenchman

1820 Bedford County
.1820 Belfast Twp

David Stephens
> **Sarah Cessna,** bn 18 Nov 1786   113/
> <Jonathan<John<John<the Frenchman
> **Son,** born 1810-1820
> **Son,** born 1810-1820
> **Daughter,** born 1810-1820

-

1820 Colerain Twp

Mary McCauslin-Cessna, bn b4 1775
wife of John Cessna Jr <John<John<the Frenchman
> **Ellen Cessna,** bn 6 Mar 1805   111/
> **Eleanor Cessna,** bn 20 May 1807   111/

5 Aug 1813, John Cessna, son of Major John, died
25 July 1825, Mary died
Cessna, Mary late of Colerain Twp. Will dated June 21, 1825.
> Probated Aug. 23, 1825 (Widow) Son William, son Samuel,
> daughters: Sarah James, Elizabeth Morgart, Eleanor Cessna,
> Mary Jane Cessna. Exr: William Cessna Wits: several names.
1825, Will of Mary Cessna of Colerain Twp is filed. Children: Wm, Sam,
> Sarah James, Elizabeth Margaret, Eleanor, Mary Jane, Rachel
> Jackson
1 Nov 1813, Came into Court, William Cessna, minor son of John
> Cessna, late of Colerain Twp, dec'd, being above the age of 14,
> now choses William Cessna, esq to be his guardian.
1 Nov 1813, Petition of Mary Cessna, widow of John Cessna, late of
> Colerain Twp, dec'd, stating that Samuel, Peneope and Mary,
> under the age of 14 have no guardian. Court appoints William
> Cessna, Esq, Jonathan Hendrickson and James Heaney as
> guardians.
7 Aug 1813, Estate of John Cessna of Colerain Twp. Admin Mary
> Cessna and George James
1817 Colerain Twp Tax: Mary Cessna 270 A, sawmill $210, 4 horses,
> 4 cattle, $1902 value, Tax $7.20
3 Apr 1828, Elenor Cessna married Joseph Gaston in Hancock Cnty, IN.
5 June 1828, Mary Jane Cessna married James C. Templeton in
> Hancock County, IN.

Samuel Cessna, bn 1800 <John<John<John<Frenchman   108/

1825-28, Samuel married Margaret Moss in Rainsburg, PA
1850, Judge Samuel Cessna died in Rainsburgh, PA
1820 Colerain Twp Tax: Samuel Cessna, 5 acres patented,
200 A improved, $690 value, tax $2.48.

William Cessna,   <John<John<John<the Frenchman
William Cessna, bn 11 Jan 1799   111/
Rachel Morgart-Cessna, bn 27 Oct 1798

1820 Census Colerain Twp, Bedford, PA
1 male 16-25/ 1 female 16-25
1820 Colerain Twp Tax: William Cessna, 270 acres patented,3 horses,
2 cattle, $1696 Value, tax $6.78
1813, William inherited the farm in Rainsburg after death of his brother,
John Cessna, Jr.
1823 Colerain Twp Tax: William Cessna, 272 acres patented, 4 horses,
4 cattle, $1512 Value, $6.12 Tax
1823 Colerain Twp Single Freeman Tax: William F. Cessna, mason,
$.50 tax

John Hendrickson Family
Elizabeth Cessna-Hendrickson, bn 17 Jan 1795   108/
<John<John<John<the Frenchman

1 Nov 1813 "Came into court, Rachel Cessna and Elizabeth Cessna,
minor daughters of John Cessna, late of Colerain Twp, dec'd,
being above the age of 14 years, now chose Jonathan
Hendrickson as guardian." Rachael married Ellis rogers shortly
after this.

George James
Sally Cessna-James, bn ca 1799   108/
<John<John<John<the Frenchman

Ca 1820, Sarah Cissna married George James.

1820 Cumberland Valley Twp

John Cessna bn ca 1789 <Jonathan<John <John<Frenchman
    John Cessna, bn 1780   112/
    Mary Ann McVicker-Cessna, bn 1783   112/
    Charles Cessna, bn 1818
    John Cessna Jr, bn 1819
    Joseph Cessna, bn 1814
    William Cessna, bn 1815
    Male, under 10, bn 1817
    Stephen Cessna, bn 1805   112/
    Jonathan Cessna, bn 1806   112/
    Nancy Cessna, bn 1812
    Mary Jane Cessna, bn 1811
    Rachel Cessna, bn 1805   112/
    Rebecca Cessna, bn 1804   112/

1817 Cumberland Valley Twp Tax: John Cessna, 50 A improved,
       1 distillery, 2 horses, 3 cattle, $155.50 value, Tax $.45
1819, Daughter Maria died in infancy
1820 Census: John Cessna, Males: 5 (<10); 2 (10-15); 1 (26-44)
       Females: 2 (10-15); 1 (26-44)   2 engaged in agriculture
29 Feb 1824, Wm Boor married Sarah Cessna in Londonderry Twp,
20 July 1828, George Elder married Margarett Cessna in Londonderry
       Twp. Bedford Co.
6 Sep 1829, James Elder married Nancy Cessna in Lodonderry Twp.
       Bedford Co
1825, Rachel Cessna married John Williams
1820 Cumberland Valley Twp Tax: John Cessna, 50 A location,
       1 Distillery, 2 horses, 8 cattle, $192.50 Value, tax $.92
1822, John will move to Coshocton, OH
1823 Cumberland Valley Twp Tax: John Cessna, 50 a located,
       1 sawmill, 4 cattle, yeoman, $124 value, tax $.62
5 June 1828, Mary Jane Cessna married James C. Templeton, in
       Hancock County, IN <John<Maj John<John<the Frenchman

Jonathan Cessna Sr, bn 16 Nov 1760   113/
        <Jonathan<John<John<the Frenchman
    Joseph Cessna, bn 29 Oct 1801   113/
    Rebecca Worley-Cessna, bn 16 Aug 1764   113/
    William Cessna, bn 21 Dec 1797   113/
    Eleanor Cessna, 16 Nov 1807   113/

7 Dec 1812, Jury of 12 men meet at dwelling of Jacob Oster in
Cumberland Valley Twp, and affirm by oath that his property
cannot be divided with out spoiling and put a valuation of
$1,340 on said property. Jury is made up of neighbors and
includes Jonathan Cessna, Jonathan Cessna Jr.
1819, Daughter, Rebecca, born 5 March 1804 had died before this census.
1820, Daugthers, Rachel bn 1 June 1795 had married Thos Hemming.
1820, Daugther Margaret bn 23 Dec 1792 had married Mr. Hemming.
1820, Daughter Sarah bn 18 Nov 1786 had married Mr. Stephens
1814-1832, Jonathan was an early distiller in Cumberland Valley Twp.,
valued at $1521.
1817 Cumberland Valley Twp Tax: Jonathan Cessna, 300 a patented,
50 improved, 1 distillery, 4 horses, 4 cattle, $1728.50 value,
tax $4.87: also, 400 A Patented, included in tax above
1817 Single Freeman Tax, CV Twp: Jonathan Cessna, tax $1
1820 Cumberland Valley Twp Tax: Jonathan Cessna, 300 A warranted,
1 distillery, 3 horses, 4 cattle, $1660 value, tax $8.30:
also 25 A warranted, included in tax above.
1820 Non-resident lands Tax Cumberland Valley, Jonathan Cessna,
400 acres, $100 value, tax $.50
1823 Cumberland Valley Twp Tax: Jonathan Cessna, 300 a warranted,
1 distillery, 4 horses, 3 cattle, farmer, $1414 Value, $7.09 tax
1823 Cumberland Valley Twp Tax: Jonathan Cessna, Jr, 4 horses,
3 cattle, yeoman, $47 value, tax $.43
1823 Cumberland Valley Twp Tax: James Cessna, 1 horse, 1 cattle,
yeoman, $16 value, tax $.08.
1823 Cumberland Valley Single Freeman Tax: William Cessna, $.50 tax
1823 Cumberland Valley Single Freeman Tax: Joseph Cessna, $.50 tax

Jonathan Cessna <Jonathan<John<John<Frenchman 113/
Catherine Boor-Cessna

Married in 1820. In 1826 moved to Coshocton County, OH

Rebecca Cessna-Williams, 1 Aug 1762 113/
<John<John<Frenchman
Hannah Williams, bn 24 May 1782 113/
John Williams, bn 30 Aug 1784 113/
Sarah "Sally" Williams, bn 1 Jul 1786 113/
Margaret P. Williams, bn 25 Feb 1789 113/
Elizabeth Williams, bn 12 Apr 1791 113/
Rebecca Williams, bn 4 Mar 1794 113/
Rachael Williams, bn 9 Apr 1797 113/
Mary Williams, bn 11 Mar 1800 113/
Eleanor "Nellie" Williams, bn 6 Oct 1802 113/

21 June 1794, Rebecca Cessna warranted 400 acres in Bedford County
1815, Henry Williams died.

Charles Cessna, bn 1762   <William<John**Rachel *Culbertson*-Cessna,** bn ca 1764   114/
> (per daughter's grave stone)   Married ca 1786
> **William Franklin Cessna,** bn ca 1786   114/
> **Rachel Cessna,** bn 1793   114/
> **Rebecca Cessna,** bn ca 1790   114/
> **Maria Cessna,** bn ca 1795   114/
> **Mary Ann Cessna**   (died unmarried)

21 June 1794, Charles Cissna made a claim of 400 acres in Bedford
County. Land is adjacent to that of Rachel Cessna. Family
history reports he moved to Bedford County at that time.
Information taken from House of Cessna

William T. Vickory, bn 1800   114/
> <Elizabeth<John<John<The Frenchman
> **Mary Myers-Vickory,** bn 1800
> **John Thomas Vickory**, bn Jul 1820

William J. Vickory, bn 30 May 1768   114/
> **Elizabeth Cessna-Vickory,** bn 1 Dec 1768   114/
> <John<John<The Frenchman
> **John Cessna Vickory,** bn 1798   114/
> **Joseph Vickory,** bn 1802   114/
> **Henry Vickory,** bn 1804   114/
> **Maria Vickory,** bn 1810   114/
> **James Ross Vickory,** bn 2 Jan 1810   114/
> **Perry Vickory,** bn 1812
> **Mary Polly Vickory,** bn 1815

1820 Londonderry Twp

William Cessna   <William<John<the Frenchman
> **William Cessna,** bn 1801   114/
> **wife of William Cessna,** bn ca 1801   -

1820 Census Londonderry Twp, Bedford, PA
1 male 16-25, 1 female 16-25
Census states he was engaged in agriculture.

1820 Napier Twp

William Cessna, Esq bn 20 Jun 1775
<John<John<the Frenchman

William Cessna, Esq, 20 June 1775	115/
Nancy "Anna" Barnes-Cessna, bn 8 Feb 1779	115/
Jonathan Cessna, bn ca 1815	115/
James H. Cessna, bn ca 1810	115/
John Cessna, bn 3 Sep 1803	115/
Elizabeth "Eliza" Ann Cessna, bn 10 Oct 1820	
Eleanor Cessna, bn 6 Mar 1805*	115/
Sarah Cissna, bn ca 1809	115/
Ellen Cessna, bn 20 May 1807 *	115/
Mary Cessna, bn 5 Aug 1801	
Rachael Cessna, bn 1821	
Joseph P. Cessna, bn 29 Sep 1825	

*Ellen and Eleanor were children of his brother John Cessna Jr. who
died 5 Aug 1813.
1817 Napier Twp Tax: William Cessna, 200 A Warranted, 3 horses,
3 cattle, $450 value, Tax $1.72
1817 Tax list for Napier Twp, Bedford County, William Cessna $430
1820 Census Napier Twp, Bedford, PA: 1 male under 10; 1 male 10-15;
1 male 16-18;1 male over 45; 2 females under 10;
2 females 10-15;1 female 16-25; 1 female 26-44.
26 Dec 1820, Valentine Lybarger married Mary Cessna in Bedford
County. They moved to Seneca, OH about 1833.
3 April 1828, Elenor Cessna married Joseph Gaston in Hancock Cty, IN.
1820 Napier Twp Tax: William Cessna, 350 improved, 5 horses, 3 cattle,
$127 valuation, tax $.63
1823 Napier Township Tax: William Cessna 200 acres improved,
3 horses, 4 cattle, $500 value, tax $2.50: also 400 a improved,
$400 value, tax $2
1823 Napier Two Tax: William Cessna Jr, 2 cattle, $25 value, tax $.18
29 Feb 1824, Wm Boor married Sarah Cessna in Londonderry Twp
5 Mar 1828, William Cessna of Napier Twp, Buffalo Run had died:
Wife Anna: Daus: Peggy alias Margaret, Rachel, Eliza Ann,

Polly, Sarah; sons John, Jonathan, James & Joseph. Exr was
William Cessna of Friends Cove, in Colerain Twp.
5 June 1828, Mary Jane Cessna married James C. Templeton in Hancock
County, IN.
20 July 1828, George Elder married Margarett Cessna in
LondonderryTwp.
6 Sep 1829, James Elder married Nancy Cessna in Lodonderry Twp

John Clark   bn ca 1776
   Mary Cessna-Clark, bn ca 1778   116/
        <James<John<the Frenchman
   son, bn ca 1813
   son, bn ca 1815
   son, bn ca 1804
   daughter, bn ca 1811
   daughter, bn ca 1803

   ca 1802, Mary Cessna married John Clark.

1820 Providence Twp

Charles (Hall) Cessna, bn 1789 <John<John<the Frenchman
   Charles Cessna, bn 10 Mar 1789   114/
   Kathyrn "Katie" Smouse Cessna
   George Cessna, bn 1815
   William Cessna, bn 1804
   Elizabeth Cessna, bn ca 1817
   Annie Cessna, bn ca 1819
   Margaret, Polly, and Charles Washington Cessna
        will be born in the 1820s

   1817 Colerain Twp Tax: Charles Cessna, Blacksmith, 1 tanning yard ,
        1 cattle, $77 value, Tax $.12
   1820 Providence Twp Tax: Charles Cessna, 2 cattle, blacksmith,
        $60 value, tax $.32
   1823 Colerain Twp Tax: Charles Cessna, blacksmith, 1 cattle, $8 value

Evans Cesna, bn ca 1785   <Charles<Jonathan<John<the Frenchman
   Evans Cessna, bn ca 1785   108/
   Wife of Evans Cesna, born ca 1795
   Son, bn ca 1811

Son, bn ca 1813
Son, bn ca 1810
Daughter, born ca 1815

Note: this cannot be the son of Maj. John who married Mary
     Fenstermaker in 1821.
1823 Providence Township Tax: Evan Cessna, Blacksmith, 2 horses,
     3 cattle, $120 value, tax $.59

Peter Morgart
Elizabeth Cessna-Morgart, bn 17 Jan 1795   111/
     <John<John<John<the Frenchman
John Morgart, born 1810

James Cesna   <John<John<the Frenchman
James Cessna, bn 22-Oct-1797   114/
Elizabeth Lysinger, wife, bn 1797
John J. Cessna, bn 1817
Charles Cessna, bn 1819

1826, List of early occupations of Bedford County, James Cessna,
     saddler, Cumberland Valley twp.

Ellis Rogers
Rachel Cessna, bn 7 Feb 1797   111/
     <John<John<John<the Frenchman
Alexander Rogers, born ca 1817
John Rogers, born ca 1819

-

3 Aug 1814, Ellis Rodgers of Bedford married Rachel Cessna d/o John
     dec'd of Colerain twp.

1820 Cumberland County
1820 Newton Twp

Thomas Hemming
Rachel Cessna, bn 1 June 1795   113/
     <Jonathan<John<John<the Frenchman
Son, born 1810-1820
Daughter, born 1810-1820
Daughter, born 1810-1820

Daughter, born 1810-1820

ca 1810, Rachel Cessna married Thomas Hemming.

1820 Southampton Twp

James Cissna   <John<Frenchman   116/
    James Cessna, bn Apr 1751   116/
    Margaret Cessna, bn ca 1778   116/
      John Clark, Son-in-Law, bn 1778
      Mary Cessna-Clark, bn Feb 1794   116/
      daughter, bn 1808

William Cisna, bn 1777   <James<John<Frenchman
    William Cessna, bn 1793   116/
    Kesiah Davis, bn 1790-95
    Henry Cessna, bn 1815
    James Cessna, bn 1817

1820 Fayette County
1820 Redstone Twp

Theophilus Cisna, bn ca 1785
        <Stephen<Theophilus<Stephen<the Frenchman
    Theophilus, bn 1775-85   116/
    Son, bn 1806
    daughter, bn 1808   116
    Stephen Cisna, bn ca 1766-1785   117/
      <Theophilus<Stephen<the Frenchman

From 1820 Census and House of Cessna.

1820 Franklin County
1820 Atrim Twp

Henry Cisna   <Thomas<Theophilus<Stephen<Frenchman

William Henry Cisna, bn ca 1780   117/
Wife of Wm. Henry Cisna bn ca 1780
George W. Cissna, bn 1802-1804
Son, bn 1810-1820
Daughter, bn 1810-1820
Daughter, bn 1810-1820
Daughter, bn 1804-1810
Daughter, bn 1804-1810

Thomas Cissna, bn 1760   <Theophilus<Stephen<Frenchman   117/
     Mrs. ?-Cisna, bn ca 1760   117/
     Thomas Henderson Cisna, bn 1778   117/
     Archibald Cisna, bn ca 1780   117/
     Theophilus J. Cisna, bn ca 1782   117/
     John Alfred Cisna, bn ca 1785   117/
     David Alexander Cisna, bn ca 1789   117/

16 May 1813, Thomas Cissna, pri, US Arty, Late Capt Grano, 5'6 ½",
hazel eyes, sandy hair, ruddy complection, 35 yrs, Tailor from
Shippensburgh, PA. Enlisted, by Capt Humphres. Discharged at
New Orleans Apr 9, 1815. This would be Thomas Henderson
Cisna.

1820 Chambersburg

Theophilus Cisney, bn 1760   <John<the Frenchman   117/
     Nancy Richardson-Cisney, bn ca 1770   117/
     Betsey Cisney, bn ca 1797   117/
     Martha "Agnes" Cisney, bn ca 1796   117/
     Stephen Cisney, bn ca 1799   117/
     James Cisney, bn ca 1794   117/
     William Cisney, bn 1802   117/
     Thomas Cisney, bn 14 June 1808   117/

James Cisna, bn ca 1782 <Theophilus<Stephen<the Frenchman   114/

Wife of James, bn ca 1781   114/
Washington Cisna, bn ca 1798   114/
Thomas Cisna, bn ca 1800   114/

1820 Perry County
1820 Toboyne Twp

Stephen Cisna   <John<John<the Frenchman   115/
    Stephen Cisna, bn 28 Dec 1766   115/
    Mary Gardner-Cisna, bn ca 1768   115/
    William Cisna, bn 1804 married Anna   115/
    John Cisna, bn 1791   115/
    Mary Cisna, bn 1805 married Jacob Palm   115/
    Rachel Cisna, bn 1808   115/
    Lucinda Cisna, bn 1803   115/
    Julia Cisna, bn 1798 married George W. Bryan   115/
    Eleanor Cisna, bn ca 1799. married John McKeehan   115/

17 June 1818, Stephen Cessna recorded purchase of land from John
    Gardner in Toboyne Twp that he made in 1796.
31 July 1817, Stephen Cesna recorded purchase of land from John
    Gardner in Toboyne Twp that he made in 1805
12 Apr 1790, Stephen Cisna and Mary Gardner married in
    Cumberland County

Aaron Hicks
    Elizabeth Cisna-Hicks,   115/
        <Stephen<John<John<the Frenchman

1820 Fayette County
1820 Redstone Twp

Stephen Sisney, bn ca 1767   113/
    <Theophilus<Stephen<the Frenchman

Stephen Cisna, bn ca 1766-1785   113/
Theophilus Cisna, bn ca 1785   113/
        <Stephen<Theophilus<Stephen<the Frenchman
Wife of Theophilus, bn 1775-85   113/
Son, bn 1806
daughter, bn 1808

From 1820 Census and House of Cessna.

1820 Huntington County

Theophilus J. Cisna, bn c 1782   118/
        <Thomas<Theophilus<Stephen<the Frenchman
Wife of Theophilus, bn ca 1782

1820 South Carolina

1820 Abbeville

Larkin Reynolds
        Sarah Cissna/Rees/Reynolds,
                Possibly <Thomas<Evans<Charles<Frenchman
        Morris Rees, <Sarah<Thomas<Evans<Charles<Frenchman
        Thomas Rees, <Sarah<Thomas<Evans<Charles<Frenchman
        Jesse Reynolds, <Sarah<Thomas<Evans<Charles<Frenchman

Mississippi in 1816

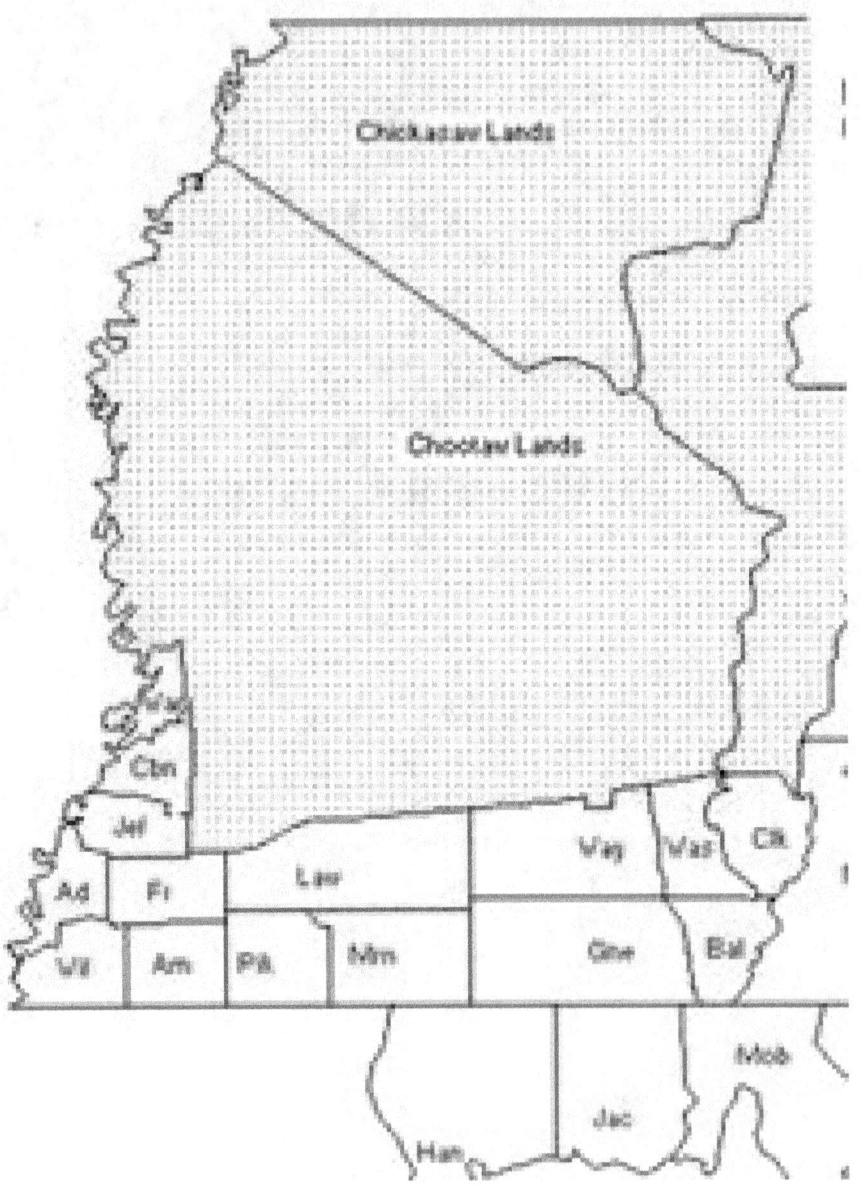

Addendum:

Arranging the data and individuals, by date and location (such as we find in the Census), a clearer picture of the family tree begins to emerge. Please refer closely to the references I have provided as you examine our most troublesome questions about the past.

Did the Frenchman come to America?

Howard Cessna in his books published in 1901 and 1931, asserted that our Patriarch (the Huguenot who brought his sons from Ireland to PA) was named Jean De Cessna. However, we have never found any references to a Jean in either Pennsylvania or Ireland.

Recently, records have been found from New Castle County, in the area along the Brandywine Creek just outside of Wilmington, DE. Until 1782, this area was a part of "the lower counties" of Pennsylvania.

You will find references to two of the Patriarch's sons (Stephen and John) in the 1730's, shortly before they move inland and take up land in Lancaster County. In the 1750's they moved again to Cumberland County. John settled in Shippensburg and Stephen settled in Carlisle.

Three Brother's and their children

Howard Cessna did a fair job of recording the grandchildren of John Cessna II (Shippensburg). But three of his sons are left almost completely blank.

He offered no names for the children of Capt. Evans Cessna. He offers only two names of children for Lt. William Cessna; those listed in the will of John II. And he offers erroneous information for the children of Col. Charles Cessna

.

In this report I will examine possible names for the children of these three men. In doing so; I utilize two tools: The process of elimination....and Occum's Razor (the simplest solution is most often the correct one.)

I MAY HAVE THE RELATIONSHIPS WRONG: but these people existed and must fit into our family tree somehow.

#1

CAPTAIN EVANS CISSNA: born ca 1743

In the Summer of 1784, (when Col Charles Cessna is embroiled in accusations of misusing the funds during the war and left for Georgia) Evans Cissna abandoned Bedford County. Evans and Charles Cessna are listed by the tax collector in 1784 as being "Among those who left:"

8 Sep 1784, Evan Cessna sold all rights to his farm in Cumberland Valley Twp to his brother, Major John Cessna. John would soon sell this farm to his son Jonathan Cessna.

On September 1, 1785, Evans and Mary Cisney purchased lot #223 in Pittsboro (Pittsburgh) for 13£. On May 8, 1787, Evans and Mary Cisney purchased lots #209 and #210 on Second Street, for 5 shillings (about $1) each. On October 10, 1791, they sold lot #210 to Margaret Millicent Hegan (described in the deed as a spinster). Margaret already owned lot #202.

At various times, Evans was listed as a tavern-keeper and a constable in Pittsburg. Although, no records have been found which directly attribute children to this couple...it seems unlikely that they were childless. Especially since the 1783 Cumberland Valley Twp Tax rolls show that Evans Cisssna, owned 150 acres warranted, 2 horses, 2 horned cattle. It further states that he had 1 dwelling, 6 white children and 4 white women. That indicates one son and three daughters born before 1783.

About 1792, Stephen Cissna <Thomas and Margaret <Stephen and Patience<Frenchman; moved to Pittsburgh. He was a widower with 8 children, or his wife died shortly after arriving. He married Margaret Millicent Hegen (a spinster of the city) and together, on 3 September 1793, they sold ½ of lot #202 for 50 £. At some point Stephen and Margaret also purchased lot #223 from Evans and Mary.

So there are two Cissna men living in Pittsburg in the 1790's. The children of Stephen and Margaret Cessna are well documented and numerous.

Logic then, would point to any other Cissnas (of that age) living in Pittsburg are probably some of the six children living with Evans in Cumberland Valley in 1783. We find these individuals who fit those descriptives:

John Cissna: John (born ca 1770) married and established his own home in Pittsburgh before 1790. In 1800 he is listed as a Tailor by trade. He is still present in December 1807.
>1790 Census of Allegheny County, page 201 John Chesney,
>>1 male over 16, 2 White females.
>1800 Census of Allegheny County, Page 51, John Sisna, BP twp.;
>>1 male under 10, 2 males 16-26, 1 female 16-26
>2 Dec 1800, Census of Pittsburgh told each person's occupation.
>>Evan Cisna, Constable; Theophales Cisna, Blue Dyer; John Cisna, Taylor (tailor); Samuel Cisna, Taylor; Charles Cisna, Taylor
>18 Dec 1807, "on this day, very early in the morning, John Cissney rode away on a light chesnut coloured mare, my property, as I have strong reason to believe with felonious intent...The said Cissney is short and stout, pock-marked, one of his eye-lids drawn rather down; had on a dark coat and corded overalls, the colour not particularly recollected. Whoever delivers the said mare to Robert Elrod at James Herron's (tavern-keeper) at McKee's Port, or to Thomas Cannon, Pittsburgh shall receive $10 reward and reasonable charges."
>This is last reference to John in Allegheny County.

Robert Cissna: Robert (bn ca 1789). In 1806 he ran away from an apprenticeship in Pittsburgh and joined his uncle in Fairfield County, OH. That same year he is noted as helping host the first prayer services in Fairfield County.

> "Wanted: Robt Cisna, 17 yrs old, 5'5", an ill look & ungovernable temper. He was wearing a roundabout stripped cotton jacket, swansdown waist coat, stripped pantaloon, fur hat, new shoes. Brand on left arm: R. Cis. Fled apprenticeship of E. Pentland, Pittsburgh, PA. Is said to have relatives in Chillicothe area."
>
> 1806, Robert and Thomas Cissna are listed as early settlers of Fairfield County and it was noted that they held the first Prayer Services in the county…and that both could and would "Exhort" on occasion.

Thomas Cissna: Thomas Cissna (bn ca 1780 d 1816) went down the Ohio River to Chillicothe about the same time as did Stephen and Margaret. In 1801 he was appointed by the Territorial Governor to survey lands in Fairfield County in preparation for sale. Thomas purchased land and established a farm there. It appears that he was joined by a younger brother:

> 1816 Thomas Cissna died while on a trading expedition to New Orleans

Samuel Cissna: born ca 1780. Following the great flood of 1800, Pittsburgh took a second census. This one was focused on the number of business people still left in the town. Samuel Cissna, John Cissna and Charles Cissna are listed as a tailors (probably working with Theophilus who was a blue-dyer). In 1801, Charles and Samuel Cissna relocate to Chillicothe, where they are partners in a several businesses and marry the Wolcott Sisters. For a number of years they live across the street from each other. Charles is clearly listed as one of the children of Stephen Cissna<Thomas<Stephen & Patience<the Frenchman.

> 2 Dec 1800 Census of Pittsburgh told each person's occupation.
>> Evan Cisna, Constable; Theophales Cisna, Blue Dyer; John Cisna, Taylor (tailor); Samuel Cisna, Taylor; Charles Cisna, Taylor.

5 May 1802, Samuel Cissna bought Chillicothe lot 176 from
    Aaron Sullivan for $15

8 July 1803, Samuel Cissna bought lot 174 Franklinton, Ross
    County, OH, from John May for $175

1810, Ross Co., OH Samuel paid tax; $3.65 on 365 ac. on the
    Scioto River in Scioto Twp.

Melinda Cessna: bn ca 1783. Melinda Cissna married Tom Jones in Chillicothe, OH on 1 Jan 1809. The only other Melinda Cissna in Chillicothe at that time was the 10 year old daughter of Stephen<Thomas<Stephen and Patience<The Frenchman.

Unnamed Daughter: According to the 1783 Census of Bedford County, Evans could have two or more daughters which remained unnamed to us.

#2

COL CHARLES CESSNA: born ca 1744 in Wilmington, DE (PA)
    In House of Cessna, Howard shares that the following is the family of Col Charles Cessna and Elizabeth Culbertson (per the descendants of Rachel Cessna & Samuel McCauslin Jr) A close inspection reveals that this cannot possibly so. Rachel McCauslin reported the following...

Charles Cessna (bn 1744; married Elizabeth Culbertson 1770, died 30 July 1837) is the father of: William Franklin Cessna (1786-18620; James Cessna (1788-1789); Rachel Cessna-McCauslin (1793-1877); Rebecca Cessna (ca 1790), Maria Cessna (ca 1795), Mary Ann Cessna (ca 1798).

    Three facts make this **improbable**. Col. Charles Cessna left a clear trail through Georgia, Kentucky and Mississippi, dying there about 1811. Also, it seems improbable that Charles and Elizabeth Cessna would marry in 1770 but not have their first child until 20 years later. On Rachel Cessna-McCauslin's tombstone, it records that her mother's name is "Rachel" and not Elizabeth.

Col. Charles Cessna of the Second Battalion of Bedford County Militia during the Revolutionary War, married Elizabeth Culbertson before 1770. In that year they signed a bill of sale to her brother, Samuel Culbertson, indicating that they were already husband and wife and no longer living in that county. Following the war, Col. Charles Cessna was charged with mishandling money and expelled from Pennsylvania State Congress. In 1784, he quit Pennsylvania and was awarded a large land grant in Greene County by the State of Georgia. The following individuals appear in records there and would seem to be his children given their ages.

John Cessna: bn ca 1762. John Cessna is listed as a private in the Militia Battalion of Cumberland Valley Twp at the same time that John Cessna<John of Shippensburg<The Frenchman is a Major and Adjutant of the Battalion from Colerain Twp. (Maj John's son was only 13). Major John's children report that he was not elected sheriff of Bedford County until 1791.

> 1777, John Cessna Jr was pvt in Cumberland Valley Twp Militia Militia
> 1779, Tax Cumberland Valley twp, John Cessna Sr   100 acres no animals
> 1 Jan 1781, John Cessna, esq, took oath as sheriff of Bedford County.
> 1786, John Cessna received land grant in Washington County, GA (land was granted first to veterans of Rev War)
> 1786, John Cessna bought 500 acres, Washington County (became Greene County the next year).
> 11 Jan 1790, Bond posted for John Cessna, Sheriff elect of Greene County, GA

Samuel Cessna: bn ca 1763, d 1797, is not recorded in the records of Bedford County, but arrived in Greene County, GA at the same time as Col. Charles and John Cessna, above. He received a land grant, identifying that he served during the Revolutionary War. He died in 1797, leaving three children and his wife, Polly.

1784 Head rights granted to early county residents: Samuel
Sessney, 220 Acres on Richland Creek
3 April 1788, petition to Govern from inhabitants of Greene
County, GA asking for a Company of Horse under
Captain William Melton to defend the frontier.
Samuel Cisney signed.
1789 Georgia Tax Digest: Greene County/Melton Twp, Samuel
Cessna
3 June 1797, Mary Cessna and John file for administration on
estate of Samuel Cessna.

Elizabeth Cessna-Milligan: born ca 1763. Elizabeth Cessna
married James Milligan in Greene County, GA on 19 Aug 1788.
Eleven years later, in 1799, the Milligan family moved with Col.
Charles Cessna to Muhlenberg County, KY. After a stay of just three
years; in 1803 they moved with Col. Cessna again to Jefferson
County, MS (near Utica).

Rebecca Cessna-Neel: born ca 1769. In 1792, Rebecca
Cessna married Aaron Neel in Greene County, GA. In 1799, the
Neel family moved with Col. Charles Cessna moved to Muhlenberg
County, KY. After a stay of just three years; in 1803, they moved
with Col. Cessna again to Jefferson County, MS (near Utica).

Robert Cessna: bn ca 1770. In 1795, Robert Cessna married
Elizabeth Culbertson. Family records do not indicate where they
married, but report that he is the last born child of Col. Charles
Cessna and Elizabeth Culbertson (aunt of the bride). In 1797; Robert
Cessna, William W. Cessna and John Culbertson moved to
Muhlenberg County, KY. William W. Cessna had been living in
Greene County, GA on land that had originally been granted to Col.
Charles Cessna. In 1803, William W. Cessna joined Col. Charles in
moving to Jefferson County, GA. Robert Cessna stayed in
Muhlenberg County, KY where his wife could be near her parents.

Unknown Son: In the 1790's four Cessna boys are born in
Georgia: Charles Cessna, Culbertson D. Cessna, James/Joseph
Cessna and William S. Cessna. Two of the boys will later report to

the Census that they were born in Georgia. In the 1806, 1808, and 1810 census the oldest three are reported living with Col. Charles Cessna on his farm in Utica, MS. There were no females living with them, just three young men and the Colonel. In July of 1811, Charles sold most of his property to Joseph (bn ca 1793) , William S. (bn ca 1791) and Culbertson Cessna (bn ca 1792). William S. Cessna is living a few miles away with the Neel family, indicating he is probably the youngest. The younger Charles Cessna (bn ca 1795) inherited the farm at Col. Charles' death, soon after 1811. When he died a few years later, William S. Cessna takes control of the farm.

The boys are far too young to be children of Col. Charles Cessna and Elizabeth Cessna. It is possible that Col. Charles married a younger woman about 1790. If so, she did not survive to make the move to Mississippi. It is more reasonable that they are grandsons; born to a son we have not identified. Unknown<Charles<John<The Frenchman.

23 July 1811: Charles Cessna sold three horses, 18 head of horned cattle, 30 head of hogs and all his household furniture and farming utensils for $200 to Joseph, William and Culbertson Cessna. Aaron Neel and Elizabeth Robenett witness sale.

22 Feb 1822 Culbertson Cissna married Margarette Robinnette in Yazoo County.

27 Nov 1819 Charles Cessna married Catherine Brady in Utica

21 Aug 1823 William S. Cessna married Elizabeth Young in Jefferson County.

1816 Census was the last reference to Joseph Cessna in Mississippi.

1811 Elizabeth Robinnett witnessed bill of sale above. Some Family Trees list that Elizabeth Cessna married John Robinette. So that Elizabeth could be a daughter of the unknown son…and sister of the four boys.

#3

LT. WILLIAM CESSNA: bn ca 1741 in Wilmington, DE (PA)

In his will dated 24 Oct. 1793, John Cessna II (Shippensburg) mentioned two children of Lt. William Cessna: Elizabeth who was under age 21 and John who was over age 21.

It is not logical to think that these are the **only** children born to William Cessna and Margaret Williamson. No other grandchildren are mentioned in the will. But we know there were many grandchildren alive at that time.

There are several people appear in the records which cannot be tied to any of Williams siblings. The dates of the people which follow would fit for them to belong to William and Margaret. Again, by process of elimination and using Occum's Razor.

John Cessna: In his grandfather's (John II of Shippensburg) will of 1793, John (the son of Wiliam) was specifically mentioned as being of age. John did not appear as the head of a household until 1798 and 1800...and in Bedford County.

It is confusing because there are other John Cessnas also living in Bedford County. It becomes clear when he is listed again in the 1810 Census because John Cessna, son of Maj. John and John Cessna, son of Jonathan Cessna both have separate listings in the 1810 Census. This John cannot be either of them.

> 1798 Pennsylvania, US Direct Tax Lists: John Cessna was owner
> of farm in Cumberland Valley Twp; 1 house valued
> at $7; 50 acres valued at $150.
> 1800 Taxables Cumberland Valley Twp listed John Cessna
> 1800 Census: John Cessna 3/1/0/0/1   1/0/0/1/0
> 1810 Census John Cessna: 2 sons under 10, male bn 1765-1784,
> 2 daughters under 10, 2 daughters 10-15,
> female bn 1765-1784

Elizabeth Cessna: bn ca 1775. In his will dated 24 Oct. 1793, John Cessna II (Shippensburg) specifically   mentioned

Elizabeth, his granddaughter by his son William was under age 21. He bequest her the farm he purchased with Wm. Campbell if she married. However, his son James used an option in the Will to claim ownership of this farm and it stayed with his family for 60 more years. No further references are found for Elizabeth. She would probably have married ca 1795, and if we do not know her married name we cannot identify references.

> Further Note: **A possibility** is that Elizabeth moved to Georgia in 1794 with William Cessna. It is reported that she married John Robinnette there and migrated with Col. Charles Cessna to Kentucky and then Mississippi. "Elizabeth Robinnett" signed as a witness when Col. Charles sold his property to Charles, Culbertson D. and Joseph Cessna.

Charles Cessna: A mystery is the presence of a second Col Charles Cessna as reported by the descendants of Rachel Cessna-McCauslin. As stated earlier, she reports: *Charles Cessna (bn 1744; married Elizabeth Culbertson 1770, died 30 July 1837) is the father of: William Franklin Cessna (1786-18620; James Cessna (1788-1789); Rachel Cessna-McCauslin (1793-1877); Rebecca Cessna (ca 1790), Maria Cessna (ca 1795), Mary Ann Cessna (ca 1798).* Again this remains improbably because records show Col. Charles as having moved away in 1784 (before the birth of the above children) and dying in Mississippi ca 1811.

A clue to this mystery comes with two references. The second Charles is taxed in Shippensburg in 1779. And Charles Cessna (too old to be the son of Major John) purchased 400 acres in Bedford County in 1784. By eliminating all of the other Charles Cessnas alive at this time, and all of the known children of Lt. William's siblings.....it seems possible that this is a son born ca 1760.

> 1779 Hopewell Twp, Cumberland County Tax:
> Charles Sisney, 1 lot value £100.
> John Sisney, £756, 4 horses (£182), 3 cows(£32),
> 2 negroes (£330), 1 lot (£500)
> Bedford County Land Records:

21 June 1794 Charles Cessna, 400 acres
21 June 1794 Rebecca Cessna, 400 acres
15 Aug 1794 William Cessna, 400 acres

Note: Charles the son of Major John was only 5 years old at this time. Major John did not have a daughter named Rebecca.

William W. Cessna. It has long been assumed that Lt. William Cessna followed his brother, Col Charles Cessna to Greene County, GA in ca 1793; then to Muhlenberg County, KY; then to Jefferson County, MS (River Homocito). This based on a deed signed by William Cessna and his wife Margaret in Greene County 1794. She did not co-sign the deed he made in 1795.

When we follow this William W. Cessna to Georgia we find a different picture. In the 1850 Census, his son William W. Cessna Jr states he was born in 1780 in Pennsylvania. And in the 1806, 1808, 1816 and 1810 Census of Mississippi, William W. Cessna Sr. indicates that he was not born before 1760. This would argue that this **IS NOT** Lt. William Cessna, born 1741.

Again, by eliminating him from other families it is possible that he is another son of Lt. William. Another reference listing William Cessna as a private in the militia of Peters Township of Franklin County; at the same time William Cessna of Letterkenny Twp militia is a Lt.; indicates the presence of a younger William born ca 1760.

It is possible that he is another son of Col. Charles and Elizabeth Cessna. But he is born about the same time as John Cessna above....and is clearly living 50 miles away from them when he is 18 years old (Peters Twp, Franklin County).

1 Aug 1780, Wm Sisney was pvt 7th class in 3rd Company,
4th Battn of Cumberland County, Militia,Peters Twp,
Franklin County. (being assigned to 7th class meant that
he was a resident of that township).

1 Jul 1781, Wm. Cessna was pvt 7th class in Alexander Peebles Co.
from Peters Twp, Franklin County. 3rd Company,

4th Battn, Cumberland County Militia.

28 Aug 1794, William Cessna of Greene County sold to Jno Michel, for £20, 62 acres on water of Oconee River. Margaret Cessna signed to relinquish widow's rights.

6 November 1795, William Cessna of Greene County sold to James Morgan of same county for £20, 280 acres on waters of Oconee River, part of a tract where William Cessna now lives, and part of a 670 Acres granted to Charles Cessna on 19 Aug 1788.

1810 Census of Jefferson County Mississippi Territory: William Cisna....1/3/1/0/0/5: 1 male over 21/3 males under/1 female over/0 females under/5 total

www.ingramcontent.com/pod-product-compliance
Lightning Source LLC
Chambersburg PA
CBHW071356280526
45787CB00001B/346